Inquiry-Based Learning Using Everyday Objects

Amy Edmonds Alvarado • Patricia R. Herr

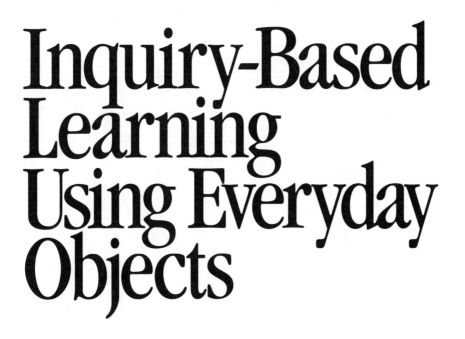

Inquiry-Based Learning Using Everyday Objects

**Hands-On Instructional Strategies
That Promote Active Learning in Grades 3-8**

CORWIN PRESS, INC.
A Sage Publications Company
Thousand Oaks, California

For information:

Corwin Press, Inc.
A Sage Publications Company
2455 Teller Road
Thousand Oaks, California 91320
www.corwinpress.com

Sage Publications Ltd.
6 Bonhill Street
London EC2A 4PU
United Kingdom

Sage Publications India Pvt. Ltd.
B-42, Panchsheel Enclave
Post Box 4109
New Delhi 110 017 India

Printed in the United States of America

Library of Congress Cataloging-in-Publication Data

Alvarado, Amy Edmonds.
Inquiry-based learning using everyday objects: Hands-on instructional strategies that promote active learning in grades 3-8 / Amy Edmonds Alvarado, Patricia R. Herr.
    p. cm.
Includes index.
ISBN 0-7619-4679-9 (C) — ISBN 0-7619-4680-2 (P)
    1. Object-teaching. 2. Inquiry (Theory of knowledge)
3. Education, Elementary—Curricula. 4. Active learning. I. Herr, Patricia R. II. Title.
LB1520 .A49 2003
372.13—dc21

                                    2002151403

03   04   05   06   10   9   8   7   6   5   4   3   2   1

Acquisitions Editor:	Faye Zucker
Editorial Assistant:	Stacy Wagner
Production Editor:	Melanie Birdsall
Copy Editor:	Robert Holm
Typesetter:	C&M Digitals (P) Ltd.
Proofreader:	Nancy Lambert
Indexer:	Sheila Bodell
Cover Designer:	Tracy E. Miller
Production Artist:	Michelle Lee

Contents

Acknowledgments

Our work with object-based inquiry began with our participation in the Smithsonian Institution's IWonder program at the Naturalist Center in Leesburg, Virginia. We have received invaluable support and encouragement in our development in the use of these strategies from Richard Efthim, program director at the Naturalist Center, and from the other mentor teachers with whom we have worked at the center, particularly John Demary. The IWonder participants from Loudoun County public schools in Loudoun County, Virginia, also provided motivation and offered feedback in the development of these lessons and strategies. We would like to thank students from Loudoun County public schools for allowing us to showcase their work. We would like to particularly acknowledge the work contributed by our students at Ball's Bluff and Sanders Corner Elementary Schools.

The authors and Corwin Press would like to thank the following reviewers:

Eileen Cannon
Third Grade Teacher
Glen Forest Elementary School
Falls Church, Virginia

Eric Poto
Fourth Grade Teacher
Ball's Bluff Elementary School
Leesburg, Virginia

Anthony Cadungog
Middle School Teacher
Loudoun County Public Schools
Leesburg, Virginia

Bonnie Horning
Seventh Grade Science Teacher
Seneca Ridge Middle School
Sterling, Virginia

About the Authors

Amy Edmonds Alvarado has thirteen years' experience in the classroom and extensive expertise in helping educators improve instructional techniques and curriculum design in all content areas. She has an undergraduate degree in English and Secondary Education from the College of William and Mary and a master's degree in Educational Psychology with a specialization in gifted education from the University of Virginia. She is currently a doctoral candidate in Curriculum and Instruction at the University of Virginia.

Ms. Alvarado has been identified four times as one of the Agnes Meyer Outstanding Educators in Loudoun County, Virginia. Additionally, Ms. Alvarado is a National Board Certified teacher in the area of Middle Childhood Generalist.

For three years she has conducted workshops for the Smithsonian Institution's Naturalist Center on the development and implementation of object-based inquiry lessons in science designed to make students more careful observers, more thorough questioners, and more inquiry-oriented in their approach to science. She has worked as a mentor teacher for the Naturalist Center's IWonder program, helping other teachers learn to incorporate object-based inquiry strategies into their classrooms and to develop object-based inquiry lessons.

Patricia R. Herr has eleven years of experience in the classroom and has participated in curriculum design in all academic areas during that time. She has an undergraduate degree in Psychology and Social Science from Frostburg State University and a master's degree in Education from Marymount University. She also holds a certificate in Technology Education from George Mason University. She is currently teaching fifth grade at Ball's Bluff Elementary School and has done so for the past seven years.

Mrs. Herr has been identified twice as one of the Agnes Meyer Outstanding Educators in Loudoun County, Virginia. Additionally, she has mentored new teachers and supervised student teachers. Mrs. Herr has been actively involved in the Minority Achievement Committee countywide, serving as the chair for two years, and the co-chair for two years. She helped develop a mentoring program that was implemented countywide. She has also been the recipient of a number of grants to further the practice of object-based inquiry teaching, which have benefited students with the addition of a museum exhibit area in the school. She has worked as a mentor teacher for the Naturalist Center's IWonder program helping other teachers learn to incorporate object-based inquiry strategies into their classrooms and to develop object-based inquiry lessons.

The making of this book would not have been possible without the support and patience of our families.

To Thomas
Emily, Brent, Lexie, and Andrew Logan
Clay Edmonds
and to Tom and Martha Edmonds

—AEA

To Tony, Jonathan, Christopher, Nicholas, and Rachael
To Tony, Sr.
and to John and Meriam Rogan

—PRH

Introduction

Welcome to Inquiry-Based Learning Using Everyday Objects (Object-Based Inquiry)

Inquiry-based learning and *inquiry teaching* are phrases that mean different things to different people. For some, inquiry means turning students loose to investigate areas of interest to them. For others, inquiry means experimentation, even if the teacher provides all of the steps and students know the final outcome they are trying to reach—the so-called verification lab. Neither of these notions truly captures the essence of what inquiry teaching and learning is all about.

In this book, we seek to promote the notion of inquiry as a process, initiated by either teacher or students, in which students investigate central, essential questions while their teacher guides them through this process. Again, these essential questions can come from either the teacher or the students. Many teachers with whom we have worked believe that if the teacher poses the initial question, students are not truly engaged in inquiry. Certainly they are! Teachers must address curriculum standards and teach specific objectives. They cannot ignore these elements. But teachers can turn these standards and objectives into investigations which, while encompassing the concepts they must teach, honor the curiosity of the students themselves. Initial questions are just that—*beginning points* for student investigation. The students become responsible for the direction they go in pursuit of understanding the initial question.

Students' ability to pursue answers along different pathways does not occur naturally. We designed this book to help teachers begin to understand how to help students learn to truly engage in inquiry. We provide guidance in using an object-based approach to inquiry which will help students become more observant, more inquisitive, and more reflective. Teachers must train students in this type of thinking and in the development of their reasoning abilities. Through the sample lessons we have provided, we hope to give teachers user-friendly models of this process. We have structured the lessons to increase both teacher and student success with the process and have provided tips on how to move along the continuum from more structured to more student-initiated. This book is intended as a stimulus for change in both teaching and thinking, and we offer object-based inquiry as a tool for teachers to add to their existing repertoire of teaching strategies.

Along this line, it is important to keep in mind that object-based inquiry is not suitable for every lesson or every concept you need to teach. Object-based inquiry is simply a strategy to enhance your skills as an instructor. It is ideal for encouraging students' observation and critical thinking skills such as classifying and categorizing. It is also an excellent strategy for lessons in which you are teaching for conceptual change. It is clear that students enter our classrooms with conceptions and beliefs in place. Although many of these beliefs are erroneous, students nonetheless interpret all new information in light of these previously held conceptions (Driver, 1989). Believing that teachers should strive to help students come to more accurate conceptions, we feel that it is important that teachers understand how this change is accommodated.

An excellent model for teachers to use is Posner's process of "conceptual exchange" (Posner, Strike, Hewson, & Gertzog, 1982). In this model, four conditions must be in place before a student will engage in "conceptual exchange." First, the student must experience a sense of dissatisfaction with his or her original idea. This occurs primarily when the student finds the original conception inadequate to accommodate some new knowledge. Second, the student must find the new conception intelligible. In other words, the idea should make sense to him or her. Third, the new idea must be plausible or in line with the student's view of the way the world works, and finally, the idea must be fruitful in that the student has good reason to adopt it (Posner, Strike, Hewson, & Gertzog, 1982). Object-based inquiry accommodates these four conditions necessary for conceptual change. This process allows students to investigate their own ideas about a topic under the guidance of a teacher who understands both the misconceptions students hold and the power found in students investigating their own ideas.

We hope that you enjoy discovering the power of using object-based inquiry in your classroom and find encouragement in the growth you will see in your students' reasoning abilities, insights, and ability to make connections.

REFERENCES

Driver, R. (1989). Students' conceptions and the learning of science. *International Journal of Science Education, 11,* 481–490.

Posner, G. J., Strike, K. A., Hewson, P. W., & Gertzog, W. A. (1982). Accommodation of a scientific conception: Toward a theory of conceptual change. *Science Education, 66*(2), 211–217.

Part I

Object-Based Learning

What Is Object-Based Inquiry?

1

When you first enter the classroom, you are struck by the utter silence that pervades the room. Students are hunched over their desks for what surely must be the test of the year. You arrive at this conclusion by observing the intent looks on students' faces and the attention that they have focused on the paper on their desks.

A second look, however, reveals that the objects on which the students are focusing are not the papers on their desks, but rather ocean organisms, one of which is in front of each student. The paper is merely a means for students to record their observations and questions about their natural object. Perhaps, you think, this is not a test at all. Perhaps this is one of those "new-fangled" performance assessment tasks. After all, the students are extremely involved with these objects and are giving them an undue amount of attention.

Suddenly the silence is broken by a student question—"What are these 'pincher-things' on my animal?" Then another—"How heavy is this shell when the organism is living inside it?"

The teacher responds with, "Great questions! Write them down on your sheet!" Then she reminds the students of their task. "Your job is to determine what your organism is and then figure out where in the ocean it lives. In order to do this you will need to examine your organism and come up with some guiding questions to help you reach the answer to the bigger questions I just gave you. Now that you have had some time to observe your specimen and determine some of your own questions, work with the others at your table to compare questions and formulate additional ones." Once again questions erupt as students eagerly engage in conversation and write out question after question:

- How does it eat?
- What is its prey?
- How does it defend itself from predators?
- How strong does it have to be to survive in its environment?
- How cold can the water be where it lives?
- How does it move?
- Why does it have such a thick shell?
- Why doesn't mine *have* a shell?

During this experience, you watch as the teacher circulates, asking key questions as students observe and examine their organisms, refocusing students who seem to have become too intent on one aspect of their animal and directing students always to return to the original two questions—what is this organism and where does it live–and, of course, to the object itself. As the conversations reach an excited pitch, the teacher determines that it is time to bring her students back together as a whole group to share what they have brainstormed. Students protest and insist that they still have more questions which they did not have time to add to their lists. But the teacher insists, indicating that there will be time to add further questions during the next phase. Student groups then share their questions with the whole class, and all the children are eager to contribute their individual and small-group questions. Amazingly, you notice that few students appear hesitant to offer ideas, and all are enthusiastically participating. As students share their ideas, the teacher fills sheet after sheet of chart paper; question after question is added to the list of guiding research questions. You watch as eventually all the students contribute to the creation of a list of thirty to forty questions—all from one small ocean organism sitting on their desks. (See Figure 1.1.)

The next day when you return, the students move into the research phase of their lesson. Each student investigates the answers to some of the questions compiled by the class. The teacher then asks the students to use this information to classify their organisms into two groups— students determining from their research into which group their animal belongs. You observe students making hypotheses about environmental characteristics of their organisms' habitats and determining reasons for certain adaptations found in the animals, and you realize as the lesson ends that the students have essentially figured out for themselves not only the environmental characteristics specific to certain ocean zones, but also some essential information regarding adaptation and change.

Figure 1.1   Partial List of Research Questions Developed by a Fifth-Grade Class

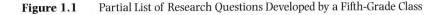

What are its predators? Its prey?

Is it strong? Fragile?

Can it handle rough water? Calm?

Can it dig or burrow?

How much cold can it stand?

How much salt can it handle?

Is it flexible or stiff?

Can it harm humans?

What is its texture?

Can it handle being dry or out of the water?

Does it like dark or light?

Does it need dark or light?

Why does it have this particular shape?

Why is it this color?

Does it rely on camouflage?

How fast does it move?

How does its size or shape determine its movement?

How does it defend/protect itself?

Can it handle pressure?

How much does/can it weigh?

THE REALITY OF OBJECT-BASED LEARNING

The scenario described above may seem too good to be true. It may appear to be unrealistic, especially given today's classroom demands and problems. It may even strike you as a case of wishful thinking. The above scenario, however, is a description of a highly diverse class of twenty-seven fifth graders engaged in an object-based science experience during an ocean study. What makes a lesson such as this one successful? What leads students to deep understandings of the essential concepts embedded in a unit of study?

One critical aspect of the lesson is the use of a variety of objects which serve as the vehicle for the development of understanding of lesson concepts. But is this lesson the result of just giving students objects to observe? Indeed students are asked to observe their natural objects, but they are asked to do so much more than that. In object-based learning, the objects themselves become central to developing the concepts which are essential to your unit of study. The objects are not merely an add-on component. They are not just used for display. They do not come with a "no touching" sign attached. The objects are *the* central component of the lesson and the overall unit of study.

Another critical component of this lesson centers on what students are asked to do with the objects. The teacher could have asked the students to conduct an experiment about ocean animals beginning with one common hypothesis and concluding with one set of results. Instead the teacher asks her students to utilize the natural objects to discover information through posing and investigating their own questions. The teacher uses students' natural curiosity and propensity for posing questions to guide her instruction. Students are given time to observe and develop questions independently, but when some students can no longer contain their questions, she allows time for small group interaction. When the excitement is still at a high level, she cuts the brainstorming time off, allowing that enthusiasm to carry over into the whole-class portion of the lesson. The class's response to the objects and their ability to utilize objects effectively is the result of their experience with object-based inquiry lessons. Likewise your students' ability to interact productively with objects will grow each time you do one of these types of lessons with your students.

So what exactly is the teacher's role in object-based inquiry? It is obvious that the teacher's job involves asking questions, but what types of questions are ideal? How are those questions developed? A third essential part of object-based learning involves utilizing well-thought-out questions which will stimulate critical, higher-level thinking by the students. These questions are critical in that they provide students with their thinking task. They are not questions for which a quick correct answer will be enough. These questions take time to develop if they are to be different from the typical, closed, low-level questions which are often used in classrooms and which do not stimulate student thinking. In addition to the critical initial questions, the teacher's role throughout the lesson is one centered around questioning. Rather than answering students' questions, the teacher's job is to lead students to their own answers to their questions either through an open-ended response question or through refocusing the students on their observations of the objects. In this way, the teacher is helping students avoid focusing on *one* correct answer early on in the investigation. In Chapter 4 we offer guidance in developing strong initial questions as well as a variety of questioning techniques designed to increase your students' higher-level thinking about objects.

Most important of all of the characteristics, object-based lessons are student-directed experiences where the teacher follows paths created by

Figure 1.2   What Object-Based Learning IS and ISN'T

Object-Based Learning IS . . .	Object-Based Learning ISN'T . . .
Using a variety of objects as central to the development of lesson concepts.	Using objects as display pieces.
Utilizing objects to discover information through posing and investigating questions.	Conducting science experiments that begin with one hypothesis and yield one result.
Utilizing well-thought-out initial questions to stimulate further critical, higher-level thinking.	Giving students answers or specific questions that can be answered simply with a quick, correct answer.
Using students' natural curiosity and propensity for question-posing to guide instruction in all subjects.	Teacher-directed learning where the teacher knows THE correct answer and THE way to get that answer.
Leading students to their own answers to questions by (a) responding with open-ended questions or (b) returning the students' focus to the object.	
Student-directed learning that follows paths created by the students.	

the students. These lessons do not involve the teacher knowing *the* correct answer and *the* one way to arrive at that answer. Instead students direct the course of their learning with gentle guidance from the teacher and, in the process, develop deeper understanding of essential concepts while using multiple paths to investigate the answers to their own questions.

WHY USE OBJECT-BASED INQUIRY?

Object-based learning involves using well-thought-out initial questions to stimulate student thinking and question development. It involves the teacher refocusing students on their objects and their questions through the use of guiding questions. It seems very different and very exciting, but it also seems very time consuming both in terms of planning and in the time it would take students to arrive at any conclusions. Additionally, many people—teachers, students, and administrators—may feel uncomfortable with these less defined tasks. Why would a teacher decide to use object-based teaching and learning in the classroom? More important, how do students benefit from the use of such a strategy?

Planning Time

Yes, object-based inquiry lessons take time to develop. It *does* take time to develop collections that are appropriate for use in your units of study. There are, however, countless places for collecting specimens and many different and creative ways of going about it. Many are cheap, if not free, for teachers; and if you just ask, many people are happy to help you. Students and their parents can be a great resource! Chapter 2 contains many ideas for where and how to begin collecting and then, later on, for adding to your collections. Developing powerful initial questions also takes time, but, again, there are resources focusing on questioning that are available to teachers. Concentrating on the higher levels of Bloom's taxonomy is a familiar place to start with developing higher-level questions for these lessons. Additionally, strategies of Socratic questioning and Hilda Taba's work with inductive questioning both provide teachers with a vast store of questioning techniques that teachers can apply both to initial question development and to the use of guiding questions throughout your lesson. These techniques will be discussed further in Chapter 4.

You *will* invest a great deal of time preparing for an object-based lesson. The trade-off, however, comes during the actual lesson. Since the lesson is student-directed, the teacher is freed up during this time to observe students as they are working and interacting with other students. Through such observations, teachers can come to know better what students need. Teachers can determine which students are developing strong understandings of the concepts that are central to the unit and which students need further guidance. The teacher is not the "sage on the stage," presenting the information to students and hoping they "get" it. Instead students are actively engaged in their learning.

Student Understandings

When students are actively engaged in investigating their own questions and interests, several positive consequences occur. First, student motivation increases as students become absorbed in their study. Second, student understandings are deeper when they arrive at the answer(s) themselves with careful guidance from the teacher. Furthermore, these understandings carry over into other subjects where students begin to make other, deeper connections. Third, object-based learning allows the teacher to differentiate instruction more easily since student understandings arise out of the investigation of their own questions through their own learning modality. Even if the lesson eventually leads to one correct answer, the teacher encourages students to use multiple paths toward that answer, and the focus is as much on the students' processing as on their final answer. The end result is that students "conclude" one unit of learning with deeper understandings of essential concepts central to the unit and subsequently carry those understandings over to future units.

Student Motivation

Although some students may be uncomfortable at first with the more abstract, open format of object-based lessons, students *do* become more and more comfortable with it as the year progresses. How could they not? Object-based learning plays on the natural curiosity about objects that every student possesses. Through these lessons, student are exposed to things they have never seen before, and all subjects become hands-on as the students explore the objects through all of their senses. Chapters 6 through 9 provide numerous examples of lessons that would be good to use with those students (and teachers!) just beginning to explore object-based learning. Beginning with lessons such as these will motivate students to further explore objects and will lead to participation in lessons of greater and greater complexity.

Instructional Time and
Improved Student Competencies

Another big time issue in addition to planning time is the amount of instructional time needed for object-based lessons. Without a doubt, beginning object-based lessons do require longer periods of time. However, when you look at the amount of interdisciplinary teaching that you can accomplish through this type of lesson, you will see that the time spent on "one" object-based lesson is well worth it. In the course of one two-hour object-based lesson, you might include skills from science, language, reading, and art. If you are working in a middle or junior high school where you teach a single subject, consider teaming with colleagues in other disciplines to achieve interdisciplinary efficiency. Additionally, as mentioned earlier, by using this type of lesson you can encourage deeper levels of thinking and develop deeper understandings of concepts in your students. Thus you will find that there is less need to keep returning to concepts which you taught your students earlier but which they never really learned with any depth or thoroughness. Students begin to transfer these understandings to other subject areas as well, and soon you will find that you're actually saving instructional time. As the year progresses, you will also see an improvement in the quality of student thinking due to the

Figure 1.3   Advantages of Object-Based Learning

Student investigation arises out of student questions and interests, so students are more motivated.

Even if lessons eventually lead to one correct answer, value is placed on multiple paths toward that answer.

Focus is as much on the students' processing as on their final answer.

Student understandings are deeper when they arrive at the answer(s) themselves.

These understandings carry over into other subjects, so students begin to see more connections.

It plays on the natural curiosity about objects which all students possess.

Students are exposed to objects they may never have experienced before.

Teacher is freed up during the lesson to observe students as they are working and interacting with other students.

Quality of final product(s) is much higher than if students complete the product just because you asked them to. It has become their product, and they are invested in it.

Quality of student thinking improves since there is no one right way to approach the question you pose. Students must make decisions for themselves.

Quality of interactions improves. Students are working together to pose questions, find answers, and create products.

It addresses different learning modalities so that lessons are naturally differentiated.

It makes all subjects hands-on.

fact that there is no one right way to approach the question(s) you pose. The students must spend time thinking about the question(s) and making decisions for themselves. In addition to improved thinking, you should also see an improvement in the quality of student-to-student interactions as students work together to pose questions, find answers, and create products.

Improved Student Products

The quality of student products will naturally improve as they become more invested in their work. They are no longer completing the product because you asked them to or because you will be grading it but rather because it has become *their* product, and they are invested in it.

At first you may meet with some resistance to using object-based inquiry from people who do not see the connection to "relevant learning" (i.e. standards and objectives). As student products improve, even the most reluctant parents, students, colleagues, and administrators will be able to see the connections between these products and the documented state and local standards and objectives. After this you can invite these groups into your classroom to see the process at work and to observe the techniques students use to arrive at such great products! Usually resistance to something has its base in lack of knowledge or understanding of it. Offer yourself and your students as models of the many benefits that teachers and students can derive from object-based teaching and learning.

TIME TO BEGIN YOUR JOURNEY

Now that you have had a brief introduction to object-based inquiry, it is time to dive in and investigate each component more thoroughly. In Chapter 2 we will begin by exploring how you can begin to build your own collections to use with your students. Then in Chapter 3 we will move into issues related to setting up your classroom, preparing your students, and developing the lessons. In Chapters 6–9 we have included numerous sample lessons at different levels of complexity to help get you started. Included are both blank templates and actual student work samples so that you can see how real students responded to the tasks. Additionally we have identified national standards addressed in each lesson. These will be easy for you to also correlate to your state or local standards. We hope you enjoy this investigation and that you will find object-based inquiry learning a valuable teaching strategy for both you and your students.

How Do I Gather Collections? 2

GETTING STARTED

Building collections of objects is the first step to using object-based learning. This part of the process can be a lot of fun and, once started, tends to take on a life of its own. Although building collections sounds a little intimidating, it will become a natural part of your lesson planning.

One of the easiest ways to begin building a collection is to start with objects related to nature. One of the advantages of starting this way is that the objects are mostly free and easily attainable. For example, we have all done leaf projects with our students in the past. To build an object-based lesson on leaves or trees, have the students bring in one or two different leaf samples. The leaves should be fresh, not dried and old. Once the students have brought in the leaves, they can sort them. How you decide to have them sort them can be tailored to your lesson plan. They can be sorted by size, shape, color, sheen, rough or smooth edges, and so forth. They can be sorted again and again to suit your class's needs. To preserve the leaves for use in the future, laminate them and store them either in a large locking storage bag or plastic container. This way, you can add to your collection each year or use the same collection over and over again. You can start a similar collection using different seeds, flowers, or flower parts.

Another simple collection to build is sea shells. If you live near a beach, vacation at a beach, or have students who go to the beach, shells make a wonderful collection. If you don't live near or visit beaches, any craft store sells shell collections to be used for craft projects. Although these are great to use for a project on mollusks or oceanography, there are many other ways you can use them. One way is to place a shell on the desk of each student in the class on the first day of school. The students describe the shell in their writing journals as the rest of the students arrive, put things away, register, or find their way to the classroom. This short writing exercise will give you an instant sample of their writing. Later on that week, after revising their descriptions, you can place all of the shells in one pile. The students read their descriptions, and the rest of the class tries to pick out the shell they have described from the pile. This is a valuable writing lesson for students, as they learn how important it is to add details, make meaningful observations, identify distinguishing characteristics, and effectively put them into writing. We have included a lesson plan for this activity in Chapter 6, Language Lesson Plans.

When beginning a unit on geology, your class can begin a rock collection. Again, students can bring in rocks to add to the class collection. Rocks can also be purchased at nature stores or craft stores. Try not to purchase polished rocks, however, since they are not really useful when studying geology. You can begin this collection before you actually get to this unit by picking up a variety of rocks as you walk around the neighborhood, go to the park, or hike in the woods. You don't need to know everything there is to know about them; you just need to pick up a variety of rocks. Many times you will find fossils embedded in the rocks, and you can start a collection of different kinds of fossils at the same time. Go through your curriculum and look for units that lend themselves to collections. Once you get collections started in your mind, you will find yourself looking for objects everywhere you go.

One of my favorites is my feather collection, which I started before the school year began. (Before starting a collection of this type be sure to check on any permits you may need to collect these legally. In our state, you need a scavenger permit which can be obtained for educational purposes.)

I began this collection with the help of my cat, who devoured birds daily and left a pile of feathers behind. Then I told everyone I knew about it, including my students. Slowly, as my collection grew, I became almost obsessed! At one point I found a turkey vulture dead on the road and watched as my son plucked tail and wing feathers from him. This would have been okay if a teacher I knew hadn't driven by. My secret was out!

Another time I was on a field trip with my students and one of them found two feathers in the parking lot. He was quite proud of them and showed them to me. I was so excited and thanked him for collecting them for me. To my surprise, he told me that actually, he thought he would keep them for himself! At this point, I knew it was time to stop collecting feathers.

Teachers from other parts of the county still send me feathers they have found, and I now have an extensive, varied collection. The feathers can be stored in clear bags that seal tightly. This way the feather can be observed without touching for those students who are a little squeamish, plus it extends the life of the feathers. We have included this feathers lesson in Chapter 7, Science Lesson Plans. Since working with the feathers, I have extended this collection to bird nests and follow up the feather lesson with a nest lesson for those students who wish to do more research on birds.

You do not need to confine your collections to science lessons. Visit different flea markets in the area to pick up antique tools of all kinds. They don't need to be large and can include tools that are not commonly used today. Store them in clear plastic locking bags with numbers on them. For this lesson, I place students in groups of three or four. Each group is responsible for one tool. One person sketches the tool while the entire group predicts what the tool was used for. The students have to justify their guesses in writing and present their predictions to the class. As they research the tools and find out what they were used for, introduce the study of history. Talk about how the present is built on the past and how important it is to study the past. The pictures are posted on a bulletin board along with their predictions and explanations. Variations on this lesson can be found in Chapter 8, Social Studies Lesson Plans.

EXPANDING YOUR COLLECTION

Collections do not have to be limited to what you can physically collect. The Internet is a valuable resource for collectors. It is also a way of sharing and expanding existing collections. You can expand a simple collection of feathers or rocks from your geographic area by downloading pictures of feathers or rocks from the Internet. By printing out the pictures in color, you now have a national or even international feather collection. Students can also use the web pages you have found for resources as they research birds or rocks.

Another way of expanding your collections is to share collections with other teachers in your school or in your county. You can also share your collections with teachers across the country or throughout the world by posting your own web page with your collection and the research your students have done. Invite other teachers to copy your pictures and send you pictures of items in their collections.

You may find other resources for collections in your community. Investigate area museums. They may have collections of objects that can be checked out to teachers. We are lucky enough to have The Naturalist Center, an extension of The Smithsonian Institution, in our community, along with a county museum. Both museums have collections that can be borrowed by educators. The Naturalist Center has a collection of skulls that can be checked out as well as other collections such as rock and soil samples from different geographic regions of our state. This collection is actually sponsored through our school system and is used by teachers all over the county. Your county may have a similar resource (and if not, you could start one!).

Other resources within the community are the commercial businesses. I went into one of the nature stores at the mall and told the cashier I was going to be putting together five boxes containing Native American artifacts representing each of the geographic areas of the United States. I told her about the objects I already had to put into the boxes such as dried chicken bones, pinecones, seashells, prairie grass, small pieces of leather, and fishing net among other objects. The clerk was excited about the project and scurried around the store to help me find appropriate objects that were affordable. She found arrowheads made from rocks from the different geographical regions and small charms made from materials found in the different areas. All the items were less than $4 each, and she gave me a teacher discount too! I would never hesitate to return to the store and ask for help on another project.

Your students and their families are also a valuable resource. If you are doing a lesson on animals, have the students bring in a Beanie Baby. You have an instant collection of animals! The animals can be divided, classified, and given scientific names. You can provide guiding questions to help students start finding out about the differences between the various classes of animals.

Although real objects draw the most attention from students, sometimes it is just not practical to own or collect the actual objects. If you are doing a unit on Egypt and want to do an object-based lesson, often it will be difficult to impossible to come up with real objects. This is the perfect time to use pictures instead. Postcards can be collected from museum visits. Students can develop questions based on what they see in the photographs. You can even use pictures from *National Geographic* magazines. The students can begin the photo collection themselves.

These are only a few ideas for starting collections. Your ideas for collections can come from looking at your curriculum and using your imagination. The study of bones can begin with a trip to your butcher, and a variety of bones can be boiled and then brought to class. Comparisons can be made between bird and mammal bones. You can start insect collections for a study of insects. You can purchase fish from the seafood department for a lesson on adaptations of fish or on oceanography. Your collection is limited only by what you can think of to collect.

STORING YOUR COLLECTIONS

Storing your collections properly can preserve them for use over and over again. The large, covered, plastic totes available at any department store are inexpensive and preserve collections. They are also stackable and don't take up much space. Organic collections such as feathers and nests should be placed in a closeable plastic bag first. Not only will this help preserve items while in storage, but the bags can be taken right out of the container and placed directly on the students' desks. The plastic bags will prevent oils on the students' hands from touching the items. A few mothballs in the plastic containers also prevent insects from destroying the collection, especially your organic items. I label and stack these containers in an unobtrusive corner of my classroom so they are easily accessible. If classroom space is limited, you can store them at home and easily transport them to school when you need them.

How Do I Get Started? 3

PLANNING IN THE CLASSROOM

The first step for planning to use object-based inquiry lessons is planning the layout of your classroom. It is very important to place students in small groups. The questioning techniques you develop and the discovery process the students go through are dependent on the students sharing their questions, their thoughts and ideas, and their answers. We usually plan groups of four which can easily be broken up into two groups of two. By placing four desks together, you not only have a group setting, but you have a good-sized work area for the students. Of course, we are not always lucky enough to have an even number of students, so groups of three or five also work nicely. A sample classroom layout is shown in Figure 3.1.

The idea is to plan a classroom with groups of three, four, or five; a central area where resources, objects, or supplies can be placed; and the blackboard at the front of the room. Angling the groups helps to give the room a circular feeling, allowing students to share their findings and ideas comfortably. Displays of final projects can be hung around the walls of the room and seen by all without turning around. If you don't have room in your classroom for this kind of arrangement, you can arrange the desks in a horseshoe shape which gives this same feeling. Some teachers may already group their students, but for those who do not, grouping is essential to the object-based inquiry method of learning.

Some teachers do not like grouping students because it does lend itself to more talking in the classroom. The closer students sit together, the more talking goes on during the day. Part of controlling the talking is your responsibility. Students not only need to learn to be cooperative learners and work in groups, but they also must learn when it is appropriate to talk

Figure 3.1   A Sample Classroom Layout

in the group and when it is not. This is not always an easy task! One of the ways I teach my students is to have a hexagon-shaped sign on my blackboard. One side of the sign is green, and one side is red. From the first day, I show my students the sign. When they are allowed to talk in their groups, I turn the green side up, and when it is my turn to talk or when they have a task to complete individually, I turn the red side up. Usually it only takes about the first month of school, and then the students know, without being told, when they may talk and when they may not. Taking the time to teach students when it is time to talk is just as important as learning how to work in cooperative groups. Another strategy I use is to change the groups on a regular basis, about every three to four weeks. This way students learn to work with everyone no matter what their strengths or weaknesses are, and talking relationships that form won't last longer than that short amount of time.

GROUPING YOUR STUDENTS

Something you can't know before school begins when you are planning out your classroom is how students will interact with each other. You can talk to teachers who have had your students in past years, but many times you will have students who are new to the school or students who have not been in the same class together before. You want to plan your group seating carefully, but you can't predict how students will act toward each other, who the talkers are, who the quiet students are, who are best friends, who are easily distracted, or any other considerations you usually take into account after you have gotten to know your students. Without wasting valuable time, there is a way to assess how students will work together beginning on the first day of school.

I would suggest not grouping them at all the first day. That means not putting down nametags and not having students unpack all those new school supplies the first day. It does mean that the students come into the classroom and sit where they feel comfortable. Give them a nametag to take with them so that you can learn names, and so can they. Take note of who sits next to whom, who has no one to sit next to, who your talkers are, who your listeners are, who is accepted by the "group" that forms right away and who isn't. Have an object in the middle of each table. Again take note of who questions what it is and what it is for and who doesn't. See who handles it, who begins to read the directions you have laid out on each desk, and who ignores the object. I usually begin the year with a group of seashells on the desks (this lesson plan is in Chapter 6, Language Lesson Plans). As the students are engaged with the objects, I record my observations. You can make up check-off lists ahead of time, samples of which you will find at the end of this chapter (Figures 3.2 and 3.3).

After all the students have arrived and you have introduced yourself and begun your normal first-day routine, tell the students you have a code word. I usually use the word "school" or "fifth grade," both of which are used frequently that day. When they hear the word, they are to get up, take their papers and pencils and sit at another group of desks. The stipulation is that they cannot sit with people with whom they have already sat. This will prevent pairs of students from moving together. After each move, continue to assess the characteristics of your students. Observe who has artistic talent, who volunteers to share their work with the class, who seems to be in charge of the material, who dominates conversations, who seems uninterested, and who has trouble working with other students. All of these observations will help you plan the initial seating of your new class without taking up valuable class time the first semester. By the end of the day, you will be ready to group your students for the first part of the school year.

You may find you need to make changes later on, but these first-day observations save you valuable time when it comes to finding out the personality of your class. You will be ready to group your students so that each group will include a variety of personalities and learning styles. At the end of that day, the nametags can go on the desks, and students will come into the classroom the second day ready to unpack those bags. Now you are ready to start planning your lessons.

PLANNING YOUR LESSONS

At this point, if you are thinking that planning for object-based inquiry lessons will far exceed the time you usually give to your lesson planning, you would be right. Planning an object-based lesson does take time. However, this is mostly true only as you begin to plan object-based lessons. There are a few ways to minimize the time you spend planning for these lessons. As you become more adept at planning these lessons, you will find that they follow a similar format. You will also find that your lessons cover a multitude of objectives, and that although it seems that you are planning only one lesson, you are actually planning for an entire day (at the elementary level) or an entire week (at the middle school level). Often you are planning an entire unit across the curriculum.

We all spend time planning. In elementary school, how much time do you spend planning each subject area? If you have to plan for reading, language, math, science, and social studies, and you spend one hour a week planning for each subject, you are spending five hours a week planning. You can spend those five hours planning an object-based, interdisciplinary lesson that would cover most of the week. Of course, you can't always incorporate every subject area or every concept into your object-based lesson, so realistically you would have to take more time to plan.

Middle school teachers can work with an interdisciplinary team to develop object-based lessons that will extend to several classrooms. This teaming particularly saves in terms of the time spent on resource and materials collection. How much time do you spend getting materials together and worksheets copied? How much time correcting papers? The time you spend planning will be saved in those areas, especially once you have started saving and reusing your collections. Much of the paperwork you assess in a traditional lesson will be alleviated as the students give their findings orally, and grades are taken as each step of the project develops, some informally and some formally. But how do you decide which lessons will be best for using object-based learning?

Before the school year even begins is the time to start making some decisions about which lessons lend themselves to object-based learning. The first step is to decide what your objectives are. The second step is to take a look at your curriculum. Which areas that you have to teach lend themselves to an object-based approach? What kinds of objects do you already have that could be used as the foundation for an object-based lesson? Which concepts have your students had a hard time grasping in previous years? Which concepts do they seem to learn for the test but then forget when you begin another unit? In which areas of the curriculum could you easily start collecting objects for your lessons?

Science is the first and easiest area to begin teaching object-based lessons. Decide on an objective you need to teach, and think about the objects you could use to teach that objective as you begin planning your lesson. Next, decide how you will obtain the collection. Is this a collection the students can help build by bringing in an object? Is this a collection you need to begin now because it will take time to collect? Or is this a collection you can easily build by purchasing objects from a craft store? You also need to decide how many objects you will need for the lesson. In order to determine the size of the collection, you need to decide how many objects will be needed for each group of students. Many times, especially if you are just starting a collection, you only need enough to distribute one object to each group, but having one object for each student or each pair of students does prevent some problems such as fighting over the object!

When starting out the school year, students need practice in cooperative learning techniques. Groups of students do not automatically work together smoothly as a group. After placing students in groups of three or four at the beginning of the year, you will need to teach students (or review with them if they have experienced cooperative learning in an earlier grade) some of the skills needed to work together as a group, such as how to listen to each other, how to give each person in the group a role, how each person's contributions add to the final product, and how important it is to include everyone's ideas no matter how wrong they may sound to the rest of the group.

AVOIDING THE PITFALLS

One of the greatest pitfalls of using object-based lessons is that the first lesson you plan takes a great deal of time. You have the collection to get together, the lesson to write up, guiding questions to formulate, and decisions on how to assess your students and determine what they have learned. Don't get discouraged!

Start out easy by adapting a lesson plan found in the final four chapters of this book. Use a collection you already have or that the students can help form by bringing in an assigned object. Make changes that fit your curriculum, your grade level, and your students. Choose a lesson that won't entail a great amount of change. Try it out on your students. Then move into your own planning.

As stated earlier, when planning an object-based inquiry lesson, you can integrate as many subject areas as you want to into your plan. After trying out one of the sample lesson plans here, develop your lesson plan the same way. Try it out on your class. Pair up with another teacher. Find someone else who is interested in object-based inquiry and has the same sense of adventure you have. Have that teacher try out the lesson. Revise it to make it better or until you are happy with the results. Bounce ideas for lessons off your partner. At the end of a lesson, ask your students to evaluate it. Ask them what they liked about it, what could have been better, what was hard, what they learned. Take their suggestions into account when you plan your next object-based lesson.

Another problem that you may run into when using object-based inquiry is that you will want to use it for everything you teach. This is a mistake! All lessons cannot be object-based lessons. There is still a need in the classroom for direct instruction, memorization, and tests. Creating a balance between object-based inquiry and direct instruction comes with practice and the use of good assessment tools. By assessing in a variety of ways and at frequent intervals, you will know when to interject a direct instruction lesson. We will address assessment tools later in Chapter 5, How Do I Assess?

BENEFITS

There are many benefits to implementing object-based lessons into your classroom. The first, most notable difference you will see in your students is their excitement for learning as they discover for themselves the concepts and facts that your previous students learned through lecture or worksheets. Students take responsibility for their learning. Because they discover information on their own, they remember it long after the lesson is over.

Students share what they have discovered with excitement which helps us remember why we went into teaching in the first place. Students come into the classroom each day expecting to discover, learn, and explore. Students are learning not only to ask questions to help them solve problems, but that sometimes answers lead to more questions! They are not at your desk asking you for the answers. They are now armed and ready to use the resources that may have gone unused or rarely used in the past. Students begin to check out resource books from the library that will give them answers to questions they are investigating without it being suggested. All of a sudden, the librarian doesn't have enough books on mollusks or trees or birds or tigers. You and your students are now actively using the librarian as a resource. In fact, you may find the librarian coming to you to suggest a new resource your students could use.

But something else is going on in your classroom you didn't expect. All of a sudden, after about the second or third object-based inquiry lesson, you find that students you might not expect to excel are excelling. They are excited about what they are learning through discovery. The group with whom they are working has begun to listen to their ideas, and this has begun to build their confidence and increase their participation. There is a new respect among the students for each other. Students who have struggled with science or language or social studies in the past are now producing final products of which they are proud. They can't wait to share them with the class. In fact, the final projects continue to improve as you continue to add object-based lessons to your curriculum. Sometimes, instead of asking when recess or PE is, they are asking you when they can work on their project! You will find that it is not only your students who are excited about what they are doing, but that you, too, are excited about their work and what they are learning and remembering.

ROLES OF THE TEACHER AND STUDENTS

So, what is your role in all of this? Students are busy discovering important concepts through researching questions they have asked, both individually and as a class. As you will find out in the next chapter, your job is to tie all of this together through questioning techniques. Basically, you are providing the students with a map and a destination, but the students are choosing the path they take to get to that destination. You are guiding them in the right direction by redirecting their observations, answering their questions with questions, putting them back on track when necessary, and assuring that they leave your classroom with the information they need to know for their future academic success. More important, you are also arming them with critical thinking skills and cooperative learning skills (compromising, keeping an open mind, and sharing ideas) that will serve them well over a lifetime.

The students' role has also changed. No longer are they passive learners. Their role is now that of the active learner. They are taking responsibility for their learning by searching for and finding answers to their questions. They are discovering the concepts that in the past you have taught through lecture and note-taking regimens. Students now have a say in how they learn the material and how they reach their destination, which is the concept you have decided the students need to learn. In the next chapter, Where Do I Start With Planning, you will find out more about these roles and how they contribute to the benefits of using object-based learning.

Figure 3.2   First Day Assessment of Students—Sample 1

Name	Quiet	Friendly	Leader	Artistic	Listener	Argumentative	Loner

Figure 3.3   First Day Assessment of Students—Sample 2

Name	Sat Next to First	Social	Shy	Sat Next to Second	Sat Next to Third	Other Notes

Where Do I Start With Planning?   **4**

You're convinced that object-based inquiry is an effective approach to use with your students. You can see that this type of learning can provide greater understanding of larger concepts and allow students to more easily make connections between ideas within a discipline as well as between subjects. You even agree that building collections might not be as difficult as you thought. The big questions, however, still remain. How do I prepare to utilize these techniques in the classroom? How do I make sure that both my classroom and my students are prepared for such an experience? How do I ensure that the lesson is focused around appropriate, high-level questions and engaging tasks?

THINGS TO CONSIDER

You can address these questions best, at least initially, by using a checklist (see Figure 4.1) to ensure that you have considered all of the aspects of planning for this type of lesson. The requirements are indeed numerous, but the rewards will be well worth it in the long run. And the more lessons of this type that you plan, the easier they will be to plan in the future. Eventually parts of the process will become second nature to you—you will already have created collections, question development will flow more easily, and students will know you as "that teacher who only answers questions with more questions!"

STEP ONE: DEVELOPING ESSENTIAL UNDERSTANDINGS

The first step in developing object-based inquiry lessons is to determine what it really is that you want students to understand or be able to do. This

Figure 4.1   Lesson Planning Checklist

1.   Develop an overall essential understanding that you want your students to come away with at the end of the lesson or unit. The understandings should be broad enough to encompass several objectives from numerous subject areas.

2.   Underneath that essential understanding, determine the specific objectives you would like students to meet. These may be content and/or process objectives, and most should be at a higher level in Bloom's Taxonomy.

3.   Review your objectives to determine what objects can be utilized to help students develop their own understandings and meet the specific objectives set forth.

4.   Begin the process of collecting the objects needed for the lesson. Sometimes you will have very specific objects in mind; sometimes a variety of collections might be equally useful.

5.   Work out a good initial question for beginning your lesson. This question should be open-ended, higher-level, and "flexible" and should be an "umbrella question," which will serve to stimulate students to develop further questions that must be answered "on the way" to answering the larger query.

6.   Determine possible guiding questions; questions that will refocus your students on the initial question and/or on the object.

7.   Determine follow-up questions to use with the group once student-generated inquiry is complete.

sounds simple enough, but it is actually the step that many educators forget. Often we get caught up in the specific standard that we must address for a state-mandated test or a particular county objective that our students must master. Determining the essential understanding that you want students to walk away with, however, goes far beyond county or state standards. In their book *Understanding by Design,* Grant Wiggins and Jay McTighe (1998) use the phrase "backward design" to address this process of determining an essential understanding prior to even considering the activities you will use in your classroom.

Let's use the example of the ocean zones and animal adaptations described in Chapter 1 to talk about what we mean. The state-mandated standard which that particular lesson addresses relates to students knowing the physical characteristics of the ocean zones. While the lesson does allow the teacher to address that standard, the essential understanding that we wanted students to come away with following this lesson was that *effective adaptation aids in survival.* This understanding is broad enough to cover numerous scientific objectives beneath it, but it also encompasses various objectives from other disciplines as well: people must adapt or migrate to environments more conducive to survival (social studies), the human body adapts to varying environmental or internal conditions (health), and adapting your message to a particular audience is essential for effective communication (language arts).

Thus developing an essential understanding at the beginning can help ensure that your ultimate lesson is interdisciplinary and thereby aids your students in making connections and developing understandings. At first it may seem difficult to tie everything together in this way, but eventually it will become natural for you, and the benefits to your students will convince you of the value of planning this way. For further work in developing essential understandings, *Understanding by Design* (Wiggins & McTighe, 1998) is an invaluable resource.

STEP TWO: IDENTIFYING SPECIFIC OBJECTIVES

Once you have developed the understanding goal for your students, you can address the specific objective(s) or standard(s) you want to use to promote that understanding. Again looking at our example from Chapter 1, the science content objectives included identifying that there are three zones in the ocean, each of which has distinct characteristics, and also determining animal adaptations which allow them to survive in a particular ocean zone. The process objectives were more advanced and included observing and analyzing animal characteristics, hypothesizing connections between those characteristics and adaptations necessary for survival in a particular zone, researching to locate information to support or refute those hypotheses, and finally classifying organisms into categories based on research as well as providing justification for the classification. Each of these individual objectives supports student movement toward grasping the overall essential understanding that *effective adaptation aids in survival.* Not all of these objectives will be obvious at the beginning of your lesson planning. You may simply start with your content objectives which you might take straight out of the county/state guides your school division provides for you. The subsequent objectives (process/skills objectives) may come out as you develop the lesson.

It is at this point that you will want to consider all of the potential interdisciplinary aspects of your lesson. If you teach elementary school, you will be able to integrate several disciplines within a single lesson or unit. If you are a middle or junior high school teacher, you may be able to work within a team to develop an interdisciplinary unit across classrooms. Let's say that you've planned to address a particular science concept through an object-based approach, and science, therefore, is your primary discipline. You want to look next at all other areas of the curriculum. Is there a picture book and/or novel that you could tie into the collection? If you don't know of a specific title, go to one of your best resources—your school librarian. Many times introducing your lesson with a picture book helps peak your students' interest in the subject area. It may also begin the questioning process detailed later in this chapter. Reading a story that ties into your lesson also draws up prior knowledge and often helps the students relate the subject to real-life experiences. Skills that you teach in reading can be taught using the same book. Students will formulate questions, use information resources to research topics, collect information for use in writing, and use available technology—all language skills. They will also develop notes that incorporate important concepts, paraphrase, summarize, and credit reference sources. Students can also describe the object in writing, being as specific as possible by carefully choosing adjectives and adverbs that help distinguish the object from others in the collection. Students might also make and listen to oral presentations and reports, including using subject-related information and vocabulary and organizing information for clarity.

You can also incorporate math into the lesson. Students can estimate the size and weight of their objects and then decide on an appropriate measuring device and unit to use in determining its actual size and weight. Using the metric system during an object-based lesson to find the exact measurement helps the students become more familiar with the different units of measure in that system. Precision also becomes more important to the students as they learn that simply describing an object as "big" doesn't really give them enough information to classify it or distinguish it from other objects.

Unless the lesson is based on a social studies concept, some teachers find this area a little harder to integrate into a lesson. However, focusing on the location from which the object came can be part of the questioning you utilize. If the students are investigating ocean organisms, as in our Chapter 1 example, identifying where the organism came from might tie in nicely with geography. You can also elaborate on this by investigating the importance of that organism in terms of the history of the region from which it came. Was it an important food source? For whom? Was it used for trade? To whom? Why? These questions tie in well with many economics objectives.

Technology is another area that is easy to integrate into your lesson. Students can create databases of research findings, and they can sort the information for different purposes. Students can use on-line resources and reference materials. They can email questions to professionals in the field of study they are researching in order to get help in finding answers to their questions. Final products always look very professional when produced using a word processing program.

Once you get started, it becomes easier and easier to integrate all curriculum areas. Planning time will increase slightly at first, but that time will be made up in other areas. You must also realize that this time input also yields lesson plans for several subjects—not just one. Additionally, because of the integration of most or all of the subjects taught across the curriculum, there will be more time to spend on a concept without feeling the need to hurry on to the next concept before the students are ready. When students gain deeper understandings initially, you also save time further down the road since you will eliminate the need to reteach key concepts.

STEP THREE: LOCATING THE OBJECTS

The next step, after identifying your specific objectives, is to determine what objects can be used to help you achieve those objectives. In our example, it was obvious that we needed ocean organisms in order for students to arrive at specific ocean characteristics. You may find that a variety of collections might work just as well for a particular lesson; you might discover that you need a very specific collection to meet your needs. Use the suggestions we offer in Chapter 2 or the tips provided in the boxes in the individual lessons (Chapters 6–9) to help you with ideas for collecting objects and building your collections. Sometimes you might actually start out with a collection and use that as an idea for a lesson which you can develop to meet a specific objective and help students arrive at, or move toward, an essential understanding.

STEP FOUR: QUESTION DEVELOPMENT

Following the "object-collection phase," it is time to develop questions. There are three general areas of focus for question development—*initial questions* (which get the lesson going), *guiding questions* (which maintain the students' focus on inquiry and on the objects), and *follow-up questions* (which bring students back together following the student-centered, individual inquiry stage). These three focus areas will be further explained in the next sections.

Developing Initial Questions

The initial question you use to get your lesson started is vitally important as it sets the tone for the inquiry process to begin. There are basically three criteria your initial question needs to meet. The initial question should be

Figure 4.2   Open Versus Closed Questions

Closed Question Needing Revision	Open-Ended Question Promoting Inquiry
Does the animal live in the ocean? (yes/no)	What environmental characteristics allow the best possible chance for this animal to thrive?
From where did the first permanent colonists in Virginia come? (England)	What motivations were there for English settlers to come to Virginia? Why would some people be motivated and others not?
Who can tell me the characteristics of a fantasy story? (I can.)	In what ways does this picture book demonstrate the characteristics of a fantasy?

- Open-ended
- Higher-level
- Flexible

Open-ended. When we say that a question should be open-ended, what we are basically trying to ensure is that our questions cannot be answered simply with a "yes" or "no," with a single-word answer, or by the student saying "I can" without the need for further elaboration. Simple yes/no questions are closed questions and will lead your discussion nowhere. Often teachers pose questions and wonder why their students don't seem to have the skills or ability to discuss them. Perhaps they are not truly "discussable" questions! (See Figure 4.2.)

Higher-level. When we refer to the need for initial questions to be at higher levels, we are talking about those levels of analysis, synthesis, and evaluation offered in Bloom's Taxonomy (Bloom, 1956) with which most teachers are very familiar. Lessons that aim toward these higher levels of questioning yield more interesting student questions and richer results than simple recall and comprehension tasks. (See Figure 4.3.)

Flexible. When we say that initial question should be flexible, we mean that the question should be broad enough for students to see it as an "umbrella question" underneath which numerous other queries can be classified. This criterion actually brings together elements of the first two criteria—using questions that are open-ended and higher-level. Asking students to list the characteristics of an animal or an environment is not

Figure 4.3 Questions Based on Bloom's Taxonomy

Level of Bloom's Taxonomy	Possible Questions for Initiating Inquiry Lessons
Analysis	How are these two animals alike in their survival needs? How are they different?
Synthesis	What suggestions would you make to the members of the Constitutional Convention for the formation of a new government?
Evaluation	How would the aesthetics of this building design be affected if different geometric shapes were used?

SOURCE: Based on Bloom (1956)

only a low-level skill, but it also provides no opportunity for the student to venture off into other related investigations. The question itself does not inspire enthusiasm nor does it stimulate additional questions on the students' parts. Asking students instead to determine what they would need to know in order to identify the environment from which an unknown organism came requires them to develop further questions in order to answer the larger "umbrella" question, "Where does it live?" Students must first examine their unknown organism to identify relevant characteristics that might provide them with information about its environment. In order to answer this initial question, they will also need to develop their own questions that will lead them to figure out what it is, how it lives in, and adapts to, its environment, and so forth. These revelations will ultimately lead students to the overall solution.

It takes a long time to correctly formulate initial questions. You will need to revise numerous times in order to arrive at the best possible question. You will be glad that you invested the time, however, when you witness the enthusiasm with which your students tackle your question and when you see the quantity and quality of student-generated questions that arise out of one "simple" question from you.

Developing Guiding and Follow-Up Questions

Once students undertake their task, your role switches to that of a facilitator, and the questioning strategies you use will be quite different. The concept of scaffolding experiences for students clearly applies here.

One of the key elements of scaffolding involves providing students with clear directions and purpose to guide their work (McKenzie, 2000). Obviously the success of the lesson depends enormously on your ability to establish these directions and purpose(s) up front, but you should be careful that you do not go too far in providing direction. McKenzie (2000) describes the problem:

> The dilemma? How do we provide sufficient structure to keep students productive without confining them to straight jackets that destroy initiative, motivation, and resourcefulness? It is, ultimately, a balancing act. The workers cleaning the face of the Washington Monument do not confuse the scaffolding with the monument itself. The scaffolding is secondary. The building is primary. The same is true with student research. Even though we may offer clarity and structure, the students must still conduct the research and fashion new insights. The most important work is done by the student. We simply provide the outer structure. (p. 2)

Thus one of the primary responsibilities you will have during the period of student research will be to refocus students (often repeatedly!) on the purpose and directions for their task. This is not typically because students get off-task or do not take their work seriously. In fact, quite the opposite is true! I usually have to remind students to continue to focus on the essential question when they become totally engrossed in some aspect of what they are doing and are "in danger" of not having enough time to complete the overarching research task. Your questions at this stage will be similar to the following:

- What do you notice about _____?
- In what way(s) can this observation serve to move you toward your goal?
- What else have you found that will help you answer your questions (or our overarching question)?
- Where else could you look for supporting information for your conclusion?
- How is this piece of information connected with other information you have found? How is it different? What does this tell you?

During this stage you will find yourself refocusing students not only on the directions and purpose but also on the object itself and on their prior questions and research findings. You will essentially be asking students to find connections within their information and between their information and their object. Through this process, students will be able to discover connections for themselves and come to the essential understandings through guidance rather than through didactic means. As McKenzie (2000) explains:

> Traditional school research placed too much emphasis upon collection [of data], while scaffolding requires continuous sorting and sifting as part of a "puzzling" process—the combining of new information with previous understandings to construct new ones. Students are adding on, extending, refining and elaborating. It is almost as if they are building a bridge from their preconceptions to a deeper, wiser, more astute view of whatever truth matters for the question or issue at hand. (pp. 3–4)

So, what questioning strategies are most helpful to teachers in providing scaffolding for their students during this independent inquiry phase? One of the most frequently used methods is Socratic questioning, which involves the teacher asking students to provide reasoning or rationale to support a decision, position, or conclusion. Typically this reasoning involves "text" support, although in object-based inquiry the object itself becomes the "text" so to speak. This method of questioning allows the teacher to guide students in the processes of extending their thinking beyond surface details to the "meat" of their research while also allowing the teacher to gain some insight into students' understandings and reasoning. Through this process students are able to link ideas and concepts in their minds and see connections between aspects of their investigation that at first appeared unrelated to them (Painter, 1996). The types of questions used in this method are also highly effective when used as follow-up questions. The same questions used with individuals during the research phase can also be used to help students link their ideas together with those of other students during the whole-group follow-up phase. In this way complex understandings of the essential concepts in a unit are built out of the contributions of all students in the class.

Socratic questioning can be organized according to the purpose of the question being asked as seen in Figure 4.4.

A second highly effective line of questioning—both for guiding and follow-up questioning—comes from the work of Hilda Taba. Although Taba developed several questioning strategies, we have found that we use the strategy of concept development, or variations of it, most often in our object-based inquiry lessons.

Concept development lessons begin by having students identify as many observations as possible. These could be direct observations of their

Figure 4.4   Socratic Questioning Categories

Purpose of Question	Examples
Clarification	"What do you mean by _____?" "What would _____mean?"
Probing Assumptions	"What research evidence makes you believe _____?" "On what criteria are you basing your position?"
Probing Reason and Evidence	"What research evidence backs up _____?"
Probing Implications and Consequences	"What are the consequences of _____?" "What does _____ imply about _____?"
Questions about Viewpoint or Perspective	"How would _____ view that?" "How do the two ideas differ?" "How will you use the answer to that question?"
Questions about the Question	"What other questions might be helpful?"

SOURCE: Based on Painter (1996)

objects in the early part of the lesson or could involve research findings later on in the lesson. Once all of the observations or findings have been recorded, students group the items from the list because they share some commonality. Typically it is better to avoid asking students whether or not they want to add any items to a group they are forming even if you see other items which could easily belong to the group. This will be taken care of in a later step (subsuming).

Following the grouping stage, students should provide labels for the groups, trying, if possible, to come up with more than one possible label. Once students label all groups, they should examine all of the groups to see if any items under one group might actually belong under another label or whether any entire groups could be subsumed under another label. Once students have completed this last step, they should undergo the whole process again! During this recycling stage, ask students to form totally new groups of items. Finally, students will be ready to define the concept.

Your role in all of this will be to pose appropriate questions at each stage of the process. How you word the questions will determine on what aspect of the list students focus and how they begin to form a definition of the essential concepts of your unit or lesson (Fraenkel, 1992). Figure 4.5

Figure 4.5   Hilda Taba Concept Development Strategy

Step	Question Examples
Listing	"What do you see/notice/find?" "What is a specific example of _____?"
Grouping	"Which items would you put together because they are alike in some way?" "Why would you put them together?"
Labeling	"What name would you give this group?" "Why?"
Subsuming	"Now that the labels are on, are there any items that fit into another group?" "Are there any labeled groups which belong underneath others?" "Why?"
Recycling	"What other ways could we group these items?" "Why would you group them this way?"
Defining	"How can we define _____?"

SOURCE: Based on Peterman (1994)

provides several examples of appropriate questions for each stage of the concept development process.

CONCLUSION

Although lesson planning will initially take more time and question-development will at first proceed very slowly, the more you utilize object-based inquiry lessons the easier it will all become! Eventually you will develop a repertoire of questions which can be applied in many different settings and will know automatically how these strategies can be used to enhance the attainment of specific objectives you are required to teach. The models and guidelines provided in this chapter will be a great support, and these are just the tip of the iceberg! There are a wide variety of other resources on these questioning strategies and many others. Use these aids to get you started and then branch out and try it on your own! You'll be amazed how quickly you learn the basics of questioning and how much better you become with the process through repeated practice. Most important, you will be impressed by the increased complexity in your students' thinking when you take the time to carefully plan objectives and questions that elicit such thinking!

REFERENCES

Bloom, B. (1956). *A taxonomy of educational objectives. Handbook I: Cognitive domain.* New York: McKay.

Fraenkel, J. R. (1992). Hilda Taba's contributions to social studies education. *Social Education,* 56(3), 172–178.

McKenzie, J. (2000). *Beyond technology: Questioning, research and the information literate school community.* Retrieved December 2000 from http://www.mo.org/dec99/scaffold.html.

Painter, J. (1996). *Questioning techniques for gifted students.* Retrieved December 2000 from http://www.nexus.edu.au/teachstud/gat/painter.htm.

Peterman, F. (1994). *Hilda Taba teaching strategies.* Unpublished manuscript, Ball State University.

Wiggins, G. & McTighe, J. (1998). *Understanding by design.* Alexandria, VA: Association for Supervision and Curriculum Development.

How Do I Assess?   5

A ssessing all good lessons is twofold. First, you must make an assessment for the purpose of deciding how the lesson or the unit is going, whether objectives are being met, and what the next step of the lesson will be. This part of assessing is for the teacher and the student. This is the *formative assessment* and is important for teaching the next part of the lesson as well as for ensuring that students are learning what they need to know. The second part of assessment is the *summative assessment.* This is probably the part you, as a teacher new to using object-based inquiry, are concerned about most. Summative assessment entails collecting data from the students to provide a report to the student and the parents regarding progress.

FORMATIVE ASSESSMENT

Formative assessment can take place at any time during your lesson. You can be the one doing the assessing, or the students can participate in the assessment. By questioning the students about what they already know about a concept, you are preassessing to determine where your lesson will start. By determining what they know and what they want to know, you are deciding what activities are necessary to meet your objectives and take their knowledge to the next level.

When planning an object-based inquiry lesson after such a preassessment, you need to take into account the differences you have found through questioning, understanding that some students know more than other students about the material you are covering. The questions you develop and use throughout the lesson will be both probing questions and higher-level thinking questions and are a great means of assessing students' thinking.

After planning and initiating the lesson, it is important to assess. As you roam around the classroom listening to discussions and observing the students' progress, you can assess certain behaviors. The rubric at the end of this chapter might help you with this assessment (see Figure 5.1). While you are making your observations, you can assess the students' progress by answering the following questions:

- Did the students grasp the concept you hoped they would?
- Do you need to follow up the activity with direct instruction to be sure the concepts are learned?
- Did the students go beyond what you had hoped for, or did they go in a totally, but no less important, direction?

Since you are assessing at the end of each lesson and using that assessment information to guide your next instruction, obviously your planning cannot be set in stone a week at a time. Since formative assessment drives future instruction, it helps to make a basic outline of the big ideas and essential understandings you want your students to gain followed by objectives that you need to teach in a unit.

Next you would sketch out the manner in which students will demonstrate understanding of these concepts and objectives followed by a list of possible activities, lessons, and assessments to go along with each part of the lesson, leaving out dates and times. Draw on these notes as you go through a unit. At the end of the unit, ask the students what they thought about the activities in which they participated. What did they like? What could have been done better? What was easy? What was difficult? The students can answer these questions as part of a class discussion or in writing as a journal entry (see Figure 5.2 at the end of this chapter). This formative assessment will be important to you the next time you teach this unit or as you teach another unit using object-based inquiry. Ask the students to reiterate what they learned during the unit or after a lesson just to make sure the lesson's objectives were clear and your goals for using a particular lesson were met. Make adjustments to the lessons using students' suggestions and through your own observations and assessments.

SUMMATIVE ASSESSMENT

How are grades taken? How do you assess the students' progress when using object-based learning? This is actually the easiest part of an object-based lesson. Many of the ways in which data is collected for grades are the same ways you collect data in your classroom now. The difference is that since the students are actively participating in and taking responsibility for their learning, they play a much bigger role. Another difference is that a science lesson may also yield grades in language, reading, and/or math. You may actually find that you have more assessment tools than you had before because an object-based lesson may have more than one objective. Another big difference is that assessment is no longer coming strictly from worksheets or multiple-choice tests that only assess lower-level thinking.

One of my own personal favorite ways of assessing is to use journal entries and learning logs. Students record in the journal what they did during an activity, what their contribution was to their group activity, whether they worked well together as a group, what the objective of the lesson or activity was, and what they learned from the activity. I also like them to think about what they could have done better and how the activity could have been better. When I read the students' reflections, it helps me decide if my objectives have been met, if the students understand the concept being taught, and if I need to spend more time on a concept. If I find that a student has worked hard, participated in the group, and has not met the objectives, then the grade will reflect that. I may try a different approach with that student, present the material in another way, and then take another assessment. Simply participating is not enough. The student still needs to meet objectives and master concepts.

When research is involved, which it frequently is, I often look for a final written report from the students. I will provide a rubric ahead of time so they know how I am assessing them (see Figure 5.1). A language grade can be taken any time a written report is involved. I incorporate mini-lessons on writing reports, citing references, and summarizing information into units in any subject area, and these skills can then be assessed when students turn in final products. In place of a final report, students can create a slide show, and you can base your assessment on the information in the slide show. It is also possible for you to assess technology skills such as producing a word processing document, using the Internet to gain information, and copying and placing a picture into a document.

Another great way to assess a lesson is to videotape it. Videotape the students while they are participating in an object-based lesson. To prevent students from acting up in front of the camera, keep one set up in the room for a few days before taping. Walk over to it and just focus on a group. Soon they will become accustomed to the camera and pretty much ignore it. You can use the videotape for assessing how groups are working together or to capture questions students ask or answers they give that don't end up in a final product. Questioning the group about their decision to exclude an answer or question can also be informative.

The class can view the videotape and comment on what other groups are doing. Often students are so involved in what their group is doing that they can miss what is going on in other groups. This can be a valuable learning experience for the students. This is also a great way for students to assess how their group worked together. Different aspects of the tape can be used. The class can assess a group that is working well together—where students are exchanging ideas, asking questions, and drawing conclusions together and valuing each other's contribution. The class can discuss what the group was doing well, and students can work toward that example in their next activity. You or you and the class can create a rubric for assessment of group work after watching the video. You can also use the video to assess interrelationship skills.

Many teachers use portfolios in their classrooms. Portfolios are still an authentic method of assessing students' progress. If you include object-based activities in the portfolios, you can assess progress according to when questioning reaches higher levels, how learning is validated through tests and hands-on activities, and how a student works together with other people in the group. By collecting the students' thoughts and questions in portfolios, you can easily track progress. Students will be able to track their own progress as well.

What about multiple-choice tests and quizzes? Can you still use them to assess students' progress? Of course you can! In fact, I can't imagine excluding them as part of my assessment. In reality, all standards-based tests are multiple-choice tests. Students need to prepare for them through practice. They need to learn test-taking skills, and multiple-choice tests in the classroom are the perfect way for them to learn how to take standardized tests and score well on them. What you will find is that students remember the content they have learned better because in object-based inquiry they have been actively involved in their own learning and have taken responsibility for it. They remember important concepts because they have experienced the steps it took to learn them and, in many cases, chose the steps they followed. With the concepts mastered so thoroughly, multiple-choice tests become easier if you just spend a little time working on test-taking skills.

The best way to assess your students' progress is to use a combination of any or all of these techniques. All the lesson plans included in the following chapters have suggestions for assessment and evaluation, but they are merely suggestions. By using a combination of assessment tools, you will form a more authentic assessment of your students' progress. This will not only help you report to parents on their children's progress, but it will also help the students assess their own progress. By taking assessments across the curriculum following an object-based inquiry lesson, you are showing your students how different subjects are interrelated and how important it is in real-life situations to become knowledgeable in all subject areas.

Figure 5.1   Rubric for Assessment During a Lesson

Name	Making Good Observations	Raising Questions	Interpreting Evidence	Communicating Ideas With the Group	Making Reasonable Predictions

Figure 5.2   Student Assessment of Activity

My students were preparing for their science fair projects. I wanted the students to understand the conclusions they drew from their experiments should only be based on observable results. I also wanted them to work as a group and to see how important it was to listen to all ideas presented in the group, not just the ideas that were popular or made the most sense. The following is an example of what the students wrote after the activity as they assessed how their group worked together and what they guessed as opposed to what they observed.

- Yes, I think our group worked together. We all listened to what everyone had to say. We all were paying attention so if she called on any of us we knew what we were talking about. I learned that you should observe and not just think. We could have let other people be the recorder instead of one person. Otherwise, I think our group worked well with each other.

—Rebecca

- Yes, our group worked together. We listened to each other's ideas. We didn't interrupt when the other people were talking. When someone was talking, we each waited our own turn to talk. I learned that you should consider every idea because you never know, it might be right. Even if the idea is silly, you should still put it down. We cooperated well. I think we could brainstorm a little more ideas. Also, we should take turns writing. We should also try to stick to the subject.

—Travis

- What I learned is never underestimate the teacher. Also, that you have to observe before you make a conclusion. Always look before you make a positive idea. Bring up ideas before you have a positive answer. So, never underestimate the teacher.

—Ryan

- I learned never make conclusions unless you observe it. You have to pay close attention to what is observed. One person in our group didn't help. In fact, I didn't even know she was in our group. But we still worked well. We wrote down everything the group said, even if it was goofy. We need to be sure to give everyone a chance, be a team! Our group did not come up with a logical conclusion.

—Emily

Part II

Lesson Plans

Language Lesson Plans   **6**

- ➤ WHY DO TIGERS HAVE STRIPES?
- ➤ WHAT MAKES A POEM PERFECT?
- ➤ SHE SELLS SEA SHELLS
- ➤ WHAT'S YOUR FANTASY?

WHY DO TIGERS HAVE STRIPES?

ESSENTIAL UNDERSTANDING

Big Idea: Investigation

Essential Understanding: Observing the distinguishing characteristics of an animal can lead to the discovery of how those characteristics help it to survive.

OBJECTIVES

Students will

- Demonstrate comprehension of a variety of literary forms; use text organizers.
- Formulate questions, make inferences, paraphrase content of selection, and identify important ideas about what is being read.
- Write effective narratives and explanations, develop a plan for writing, and use available technology.
- Use information resources to research a topic, construct questions about a topic, and collect information.
- Listen, draw conclusions, and share responses, and summarize information gathered in group activities.
- Demonstrate comprehension of a variety of literary forms; locate information to support opinions, predictions, and conclusions; prioritize information.
- Skim materials to develop a general overview of content or to locate specific information; organize and record information on charts, maps, and graphs.

MATERIALS

For this lesson you will need

- A large, realistic-size stuffed tiger or other animal
- Large box the stuffed animal will fit into
- Large poster paper
- Reference books about animals, tigers
- Materials for reproducing some of the distinguishing characteristics of the animal, such as fake fur and Velcro (optional)

Figure 6.1 Sources for Objects: Tigers

For this lesson, I purchased a large, realistic-size tiger (which is our school mascot) at a discount toy store. You may already have a life-size mascot at your school you can use, or ask other teachers at the school for a life-size animal. It is a lot more fun if the animal is life-size or colored realistically, which makes the lesson more meaningful since observing the animal's characteristics is part of the lesson. A large, poster-size picture of the animal would also work, if necessary.

- A large collection of reference books and Internet access if available
- Materials to help make the display interesting (such as fake fur of the animal, Velcro to demonstrate the roughness of the tongue, etc.)
- A computer and program that can be used to display the slide show the students create to go along with the display

TIME REQUIRED

I spent about three weeks on this project. The first week the students spend guessing what animal is hidden in the box, which helps build excitement for the project. No class time is spent during this week. During the second week, students make observations and pose questions they want answered. The questions are grouped into researchable categories, and students choose the subject they wish to research and create a display. The third week is spent researching and creating the display and page for the slide show. The display is then placed in a busy location within the school. You may find you need to spend more time on the research part of the lesson. I had already pulled books from the school library and the public library and placed them in the classroom to save a little time.

PROCEDURE

1. Place a life-size tiger or other animal into a box and place it in a central location. Place a clipboard with a pencil and a paper for predictions next to the box. Have students predict what might be in the box and give a reason for their prediction (see Figure 6.2).

2. Each day for four days, add a clue to the outside of the box to pique student interest and help students determine what the animal in the

Figure 6.2

NAME/TEACHER	GUESS	WHY DO YOU THINK SO?

box might be, such as "I leave pugmarks wherever I go" (see Figure 6.3). On the fifth day, read the predictions. Take a class vote as to what the most reasonable prediction might be. Then uncover the animal.

3. Working in small groups, students should make observations about the animal.

4. Working as a class, the observations should be shared and listed on chart paper.

Figure 6.3

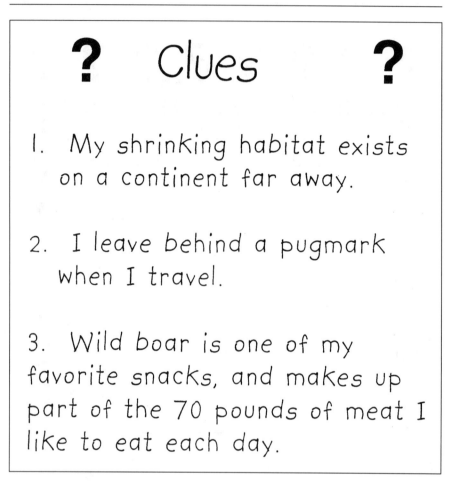

? Clues ?

1. My shrinking habitat exists on a continent far away.

2. I leave behind a pugmark when I travel.

3. Wild boar is one of my favorite snacks, and makes up part of the 70 pounds of meat I like to eat each day.

5. Again working in small groups, a list of questions the students would like to have answered should be generated. The lists of questions should then be recorded on chart paper.

6. Transfer the list of questions to a worksheet (see Figure 6.4).

7. In small groups, students should decide on some overall categories to group the questions into, such as physical features, habitat, food gathering, reproduction, raising young. Once the categories are established, the groups should work to group the questions into the categories. Give each group a large piece of chart paper with the categories written on it. Groups will write which questions they placed into which categories (see Figure 6.5).

8. Completed charts will be taped to the blackboard. The groups will discuss why they grouped the questions the way they did. The class

Figure 6.4   Grouping Questions for Tiger Mania Worksheet

---

1. Do tigers like loud noises?
2. Where do tigers live?
3. When did the first Siberian Tigers come around?
4. Why do tigers have stripes?
5. Do tigers like people around them?
6 How tall can tigers get?
7, What were the first tigers on earth?
8. How big can tigers get?
9. Do tigers eat other tigers?
10. How many species of tigers are there?
11. Are tigers smart?
12. How much meat do tigers eat a day?
13, How and why have tigers become endangered?
14. How long do tigers live?
15. Are tigers good day and night hunters?
16. Why do tigers have a mane?
17. What role does the father tiger play?
18. When do tigers sleep?
19. How are males and females different?
20. Do tigers communicate with humans?
21. How fast can tigers run?
22. Do animals eat tigers?
23. What kinds of temperatures can tigers handle?
24. What do tigers do all day?
25. Why do tigers have white stomachs? Do they all have white stomachs?
26. How many tigers are left in the wild?
27. Who was the first person to see a tiger?
28. Do tigers climb trees?
29. How many stripes can a tiger have?
30. Do tigers eat their babies?

(Continued)

Figure 6.4 (Continued)

---

31. How do tigers protect their cubs?

32. Why is the underside of tigers' feet white?

33. Which animals are tiger predators?

34. How often do tigers have babies?

35. At what age do cubs leave the mother?

36. Why are there white tigers? Are they different? Are they more endangered?

37. Do tigers like water?

38. Do tigers purr?

39. Why do tigers have a hard tongue?

40. Do all tigers eat meat? Do they eat anything else?

41. Are their stripes always black?

42. How big is a tiger's heart? A paw print? A brain?

43. How long can a tiger's tail be?

---

will come to a consensus on how the questions could be grouped, and a master list will be generated and copied for each group. Grouping the questions should make research much easier for the students.

9. The whole class will discuss how to research the questions using the table of contents, the index, and glossaries and review the resources available for use.

10. Each group will decide on a category to research and each student in the group will choose a question to answer.

11. Students will be told to create a hands-on museum exhibit based on the animal. Students will be responsible for choosing a topic for an exhibit they will create to answer the questions they are researching. Provide your students with a list of supplies they will need, as well as instructions to follow in creating the exhibit (see Figure 6.6). Students will also need to create a page of information based on their findings to be placed into a slide show to accompany the exhibit. Some ideas:

- A list of fun facts
- Duplicate the habitat and surround the animal with it
- Create a footprint to scale

Figure 6.5

Tiger Mania

Where it is found	
Habitat	
Size	
Weight	
Predators	
Prey/Food	
Endangered Status	
Interesting Facts	
Inquiry Question Answered	
Unanswered Inquiry Question	

- Using fake fur, create a pelt of actual size
- Using Velcro, create the tongue of the tiger
- Create a crossword puzzle with facts about the tiger
- Create a food web and place the animal in it

Figure 6.6

Dear Ashley and Josh,

You have chosen to do a display of a tiger pelt for your museum project. For this project you will need to:

> *Research the fur of tigers, and how people use tiger pelts
> *Write a note to Mrs. Herr asking her to buy tiger fabric
> *Create a pattern for the pelt on large white paper, being sure it is the appropriate size.
> *Trace the pattern onto the fabric and cut it out
> *Create an informational page in AppleWorks for the display and for the slide show.
> *Save your page to the TigerQuest slide show folder in Group Shared Folder

All work must be approved by either Mrs. Hale or Mrs. Herr before the actual pages are put together. In other words, you will need to plan the project out ahead of time.   Good Luck!

---

12. After students have developed their projects and a group of students have put the slide show together, students will share their findings with the class (see Figures 6.7 and 6.8). A hands-on museum display of their work will be put up in the hall with the tiger as the focal point. A computer will also be placed in the hall to display the slide show created by the students.

DISCUSSION QUESTIONS

1. How do the characteristics of the tiger (animal) distinguish it from other animals?

2. How do those characteristics aid in its survival?

3. What have humans "borrowed" from the tiger (animal) to aide in our survival?

4. How does grouping research requirements help find the information you are looking for?

Figure 6.7

Introduction

Welcome to the Balls Bluff Elementary museum exhibit on The Siberian Tiger produced by Mrs. Herr's & Mrs. Hale's fifth grade reading class. We will include information about the tiger's eye, paw prints, differences between human and tiger skulls and tiger cubs, crossword puzzles, the tongue of the tiger, and many more interesting facts. We have worked very hard on this project. We hope you enjoy learning about Siberian Tigers.

EVALUATION

Students will be informally evaluated on

- Participation
- Staying on task
- Using resource materials effectively

Figure 6.8

> ## Tiger Tongue
>
> The tiger's tongue is used for eating, grooming, and lapping. Sometimes the tiger's tongue will be used for licking meat off of predators bones. The reason tigers can eat rotting flesh is because they have few taste buds and they can't taste it. The tiger's tongue has points facing backwards so the tiger can grip into things. Tigers lick their fur almost every day.

The formal evaluation will be the final project that will be evaluated for completeness:

- Does the project answer the assigned question?
- Were resources cited correctly?
- Is the final project attractive, and does it provoke inquiry?
- Is the page for the slide show accurate, and does it show that research was paraphrased, not simply copied?
- Is spelling and punctuation correct?

EXTENSIONS AND MODIFICATIONS

This activity could be integrated into a science unit on mammals. Other animals could also be included and comparisons could be made. This could be a yearlong project with animals from different kingdoms being researched and the museum exhibit expanded with each addition.

SUGGESTED READINGS AND RESOURCES

Baker, K. (1990). *Who is the beast?* San Diego, CA: Harcourt.

Chancellor, D. (2000). *Tiger tales and big cat stories.* New York: DK.

DuTemple, L. A. (1996). *Tigers.* Minneapolis, MN: Lerner.

Root, P. (1985). *Moon tiger.* New York: Holt.

Urquhart, J. C. (1990). *Lions and tigers and leopards: The big cats.* Washington, DC: National Geographic.

Wex, J. B. (1990) *Big cats.* Mankato, MN: Creative Education.

VOCABULARY

adaptations: the characteristics that help something survive or adapt to the environment

distinguishing characteristics: the characteristics that make something unique and different

habitat: the environment in which something lives

ACADEMIC STANDARDS

Grade Level: 3–8

National Language Standards

Uses the general skills and strategies of the writing process (Writing 1)

Uses grammatical and mechanical conventions in written compositions (Writing 3)

Gathers and uses information for research purposes (Writing 4)

Social Studies:

Uses maps and other geographic representations, tools, and technologies to acquire, process, and report information (Geography 1)

Science:

Knows that living organisms have distinct structures and body systems that serve specific functions in growth, survival, and reproduction (NS 5–8.3)

Knows that scientists use different kinds of investigations (e.g., naturalistic observation of things or events, data collections,) depending on the questions they are trying to answer (NS 5–8.1)

WHAT MAKES A POEM PERFECT?

ESSENTIAL UNDERSTANDING

Big Idea: Value

Essential Understanding(s): Aesthetic value is a matter of personal perspective; language characteristics contribute to aesthetic value.

OBJECTIVES

Students will

- Read a variety of poetry samples deemed "classics."
- Respond to poetry emotionally.
- Develop a rubric for evaluating poetry.

MATERIALS

For this lesson you will need

- A variety of printed poetry samples considered "classics"
- Chart paper
- Markers

Figure 6.9   Sources for Objects: Poetry

You probably have lots of poetry books that contain your favorite poems. You can type these up yourself and provide copies to the students. There are also numerous excellent websites with poetry samples on them (for example, http://www.poetry.com/greatestpoems/list.asp). Be sure to choose poems that are considered classics in the field such as works by: Dickinson, Wordsworth, Frost, Blake, Cummings, Angelou, Brooks, and Browning. I try to avoid using too many of the more modern, well-known poems by such poets as Silverstein or Prelutsky, not because they are "bad" poems but because the classic poems contain more of the literary elements I am responsible for teaching.

TIME REQUIRED

The time required for this lesson will vary based on the number of poems you select for students to work with and the amount of time you want to give them to read the poetry. I usually provide about fifteen to twenty poems for student perusal and typically provide them with about forty-five minutes to an hour just to read through the poems, determine their favorites, and think about the features of the poem that make it appealing to them. I usually complete the discussion and rubric development the following day, again in a forty-five-minute to an hour class period.

PROCEDURE

1. Print out several poems that are considered classics. Be sure to choose a variety of types of poems—some that rhyme and some that don't, some that are very short and some that have several clear stanzas, some with refrains, and some without. Also be sure that the subjects of the poems are varied—animals, seasons, holidays, and so forth—so that something will appeal to each child. I prepare packets containing fifteen to twenty poems for each table of students.

Figure 6.10   Poetry Selection

You may feel that many classic poems are too difficult for your children to comprehend. Obviously, the poems you choose should be geared to the level of student you are teaching. However, I do not worry if the poems I have chosen contain some words that the children may not know. In this lesson I am most concerned with the students' emotional reaction to the poem—how it feels to them, the sounds they take away from it, how they respond to the look of the poem or the way it is formatted. Of course, too many unfamiliar words will frustrate the students, and this should certainly be avoided. However, don't avoid a poem because it contains difficult words. One of the poems most frequently selected as a "favorite" by my fifth graders is "The Tyger" by William Blake, and it contains numerous difficult words. The students usually indicate that they like how "intense" the poem feels.

2. Give students ample time to read through the poems. Ask them to focus on the feelings the poems evoke and how they believe the poet created those feelings. They should read through all of the poems and choose a favorite poem from the collection that they will share with the class.

3. After students have had the opportunity to select their favorite poem, ask students to share their choices and the rationale behind their choices. While students are sharing, write the reasons for their choices on the board.

4. Once students have shared, you should have quite a large list of characteristics on the board. Ask students which ones could be grouped together under a more general heading. For example, items such as repetition of words, repetition of sounds, and onomatopoeia (although the students won't phrase them quite that way!) could all be grouped under something like "sound appeal." On a piece of chart paper, record these general characteristics as representative of a "3" poem. This will be the model or standard to which all future poems—both those students read and those that they write—will be compared.

Figure 6.11 The Language of Poetry

I do make a point of using the correct literary term for aspects of the poems that students mention. If students say that they like the way the poet uses words that sound like a bee, I put the word onomatopoeia on the board and explain what that means. In this way, students begin to become familiar with the terms we will be studying throughout the year.

5. After creating the "3" component of the poetry rubric, take out another piece of chart paper and have the students tell you what the opposite end of the spectrum would look like. Write these characteristics on the chart paper, labeling it as representative of a "1" poem. The same process is used to arrive at the characteristics of a "2" poem which would fall somewhere in between the two extremes.

6. This rubric is the final product of this lesson and will be used repeatedly throughout the year when students evaluate poems they are reading or writing. As I teach poetry terms throughout the year (alliteration, assonance, onomatopoeia, etc.), I return to the student-generated rubric and point out where these specific elements would occur on the rubric (see rubric at end of lesson).

Figure 6.12 Value of Poetry

Throughout the rubric development process, the teacher should stress that the reason that our society values these poems as "classics" is that they contain a wide variety of the positive characteristics they have been noticing. Also stress, however, that not everyone will like every poem. Aesthetic value depends on the perspective of the person reading the poem.

ADAPTATIONS

The most obvious adaptation to make is in the selection of the poems. There are a wide range of levels of poems, and you should be able to find simpler poems to use with lower-level readers and more complex poems for upper-level readers, regardless of the grade level. It is a good idea to mix them up for heterogeneous classrooms. Provide a range of poems in the packets for students to read through.

DISCUSSION QUESTIONS

When starting the students off on the process of reading through the poems, it is a good idea to make the directions very general. I simply ask the students to focus on the way(s) the poem makes them feel and to look at possible ways they think the poet created that feeling. I don't give them a lot of guidance in terms of what to look for at this point.

During the rubric development, I will frequently use guiding questions to help reluctant students identify specific elements of the poem that "back up" what they feel from the poem. The following questions are helpful in doing this:

1. What types of words does the poet use?

2. What kinds of formatting changes emphasize certain words (underline, bold, all caps)?

3. How has the poet used the space around the words? placement of words on the page?

4. What do you mean by *(e.g., intense)*_____? What words sounded *(e.g., intense)* _____ to you?

ASSESSMENT AND EVALUATION

Although I do not do any formal evaluation here, there are lots of opportunities for informal assessment.

- Selection of favorite poems involves literary discrimination and developing a rationale for their choices.
- Orally sharing their choices and rationales is good oral communication practice.
- Categorizing poetry characteristics and labeling the resulting grouping is a higher-level thinking skill.

Figure 6.13

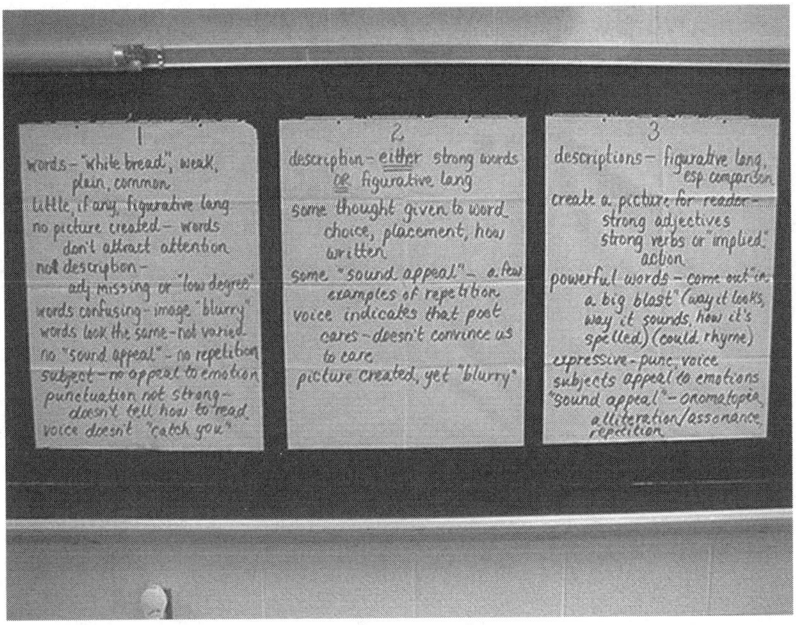

Formal evaluation does come in later when students use the rubric to evaluate other poems, both those they read and those they write.

- Students could use the rubric criteria and write a paragraph arguing that a particular poem is or is not a "3" poem.
- They can also use the rubric in peer writing groups to help with revision.

EXTENSIONS AND MODIFICATIONS

- Have small groups of students develop a rubric prior to the whole class coming back together. After they have each read the poems and selected a favorite, they could use the above-listed procedure within their small group. Then all of the groups could come together to join their ideas into a class poetry rubric.

- Following the rubric development, have students bring in a favorite poem from home that they feel displays the characteristics of a "3" poem. These poems could be put on transparencies and shown on the overhead or xeroxed for everyone. Class discussion could center around evaluating the poems using the rubric.

SUGGESTED READINGS AND RESOURCES

Ainsworth, L. & Christinson, J. (1998). *Student-generated rubrics: An assessment model to help all students succeed.* Orangeburg, NY: Seymour Publications.

Skylight Professional Development Video Series (Producer). (2000). *Constructing performance rubrics* [videotape]. (Available from Saint Xavier University, Chicago).

Heard, G. (1999). *Awakening the heart: Exploring poetry in elementary and middle school.* Portsmouth, NH: Heinemann Publishers.

Hopkins, L. B. (1998). *Pass the poetry, please!* (3rd ed.). New York: HarperCollins.

Rickards, D. & Cheek, E. (1999). *Designing rubrics for K6 classroom assessment.* Norwood, MA: Christopher-Gordon Publishers.

VOCABULARY

alliteration: repetition of consonant sounds (usually at the beginnings of words)

assonance: repetition of vowel sounds (usually at the beginnings of words)

onomatopoeia: words that are intended to represent a sound (e.g., buzzzzz)

rubric: specified guidelines for what particular levels of performance should look like or be like

ACADEMIC STANDARDS

Grade Level: 3–8

Language

Analyzing poems for positive characteristics (ENG.K–12.3 Evaluation Strategies)

Sharing rationale for poetry choices (ENG.K–12.4 Communication Skills)

Using knowledge of literary conventions to defend choices (ENG.K–12.6 Applying Knowledge)

Writing to defend a poem as "3" or not (ENG.K–12.5 Communication Strategies)

SHE SELLS SEA SHELLS

ESSENTIAL UNDERSTANDING

Big Idea: Descriptive Writing, Investigation

Essential Understanding: Observing the distinguishing characteristics of an object and describing those characteristics can lead to the collection of data necessary to investigate the object and answer questions raised about it.

OBJECTIVES

Students will

- Demonstrate comprehension of a variety of literary forms, use text organizers, formulate questions, make inferences, paraphrase content of selection, and identify important ideas about what is being read.
- Write effective descriptions, develop a plan for writing, and use available technology.
- Use information resources to research a topic, construct questions about a topic, and collect information.
- Demonstrate comprehension of a variety of literary forms, locate information to support opinions, predictions, and conclusions, and prioritize information.
- Skim materials to develop a general overview of content or to locate specific information; organize and record information on chart.

MATERIALS

For this lesson you will need

- Any collection of objects, preferably from a unit you will be investigating (such as seashells, plants, beads, etc.)
- Reference books about the objects in your collection

TIME REQUIREMENTS

The length of this lesson depends on how far you take it. If you use this solely as a writing lesson, it can take two or three language classes, one for

Figure 6.14   Sources for Objects: Shells

For this lesson, I used a collection of shells because we teach a very large unit on oceans and ocean life. I also chose shells because at first glance, they are very similar, yet they are distinctly different. I wanted the students to understand how important it is to find the characteristics of an object that make it different from other objects, and hoped this lesson would carry over to the importance of including specific details when writing a narrative story and when making observations in science. I collected shells at a shell shop at the beach, but they are also available at craft supply stores.

the initial writing, one for sharing what has been written, and one for revisions. If you decide to continue this lesson doing research, then it could take another two or three class periods.

PROCEDURE

1. Leave similar objects, such as seashells, on the students' desks.

2. Students will describe the object, being sure to include the distinguishing characteristics that set it apart from the other objects. After they have described the object, they will generate a list of questions they would like answered about the object.

3. When students are done writing, collect all the objects and place them in a central location where all the students can see them.

4. Collect the descriptions the students have written.

5. Read the descriptions aloud. After each description, have students pick out the object that was being described. If an object was not identified, talk about the object's distinguishing features that could have been included in the description. This discussion might include adjectives and how they make identification easier. Measuring an object, rather than calling it large or small, is important in observing the object since specific size is a distinguishing feature.

6. Generate a list of questions the students would like answered.

7. Give the written descriptions back to the students. Have students revise descriptions as necessary to include distinguishing characteristics.

8. Place reference materials in a central location. Have websites available to help students begin to answer questions about their objects.

9. The whole class will discuss how to research the questions using the table of contents, the index, and glossaries and review the resources available for use.

10. Students will research their objects, answering their questions, and write a report of their findings. They will cite resources used.

11. The objects and the reports will be displayed for other students to read.

12. Students will record what they learned from this activity in a learning journal, or letter to the teacher or another student.

DISCUSSION QUESTIONS

1. How do the characteristics of the object distinguish it from the other objects?

2. How do those characteristics aid in its survival?

3. What are shells made of? Why do mollusks need shells?

4. Are there any other animals that use shells for protection? Are they made the same way?

Figure 6.15

Seashell

First Draft

The shell is smooth in the middle. It has a few big bumps. The shell is like a spiral. There's one bnig hole that goes through the center. There's a little hole on the side. It's tan, white, and gray on the tip. There's many little ridges. It's mostly a white color. It's pretty big.

Final Copy

My seashell is about 3 1/2 inches long. It is made up of a big spiral. The end of the spiral is flat. It's a grayish purple color. The inside of the shell is smooth and white. There are basically four times the spiral winds around the shell. Near the small end of the spiral is a tiny hole. The outside of the shell is mostly white with many faint brown lines. There are many points along the spiral. On the smaller tip of the spiral there is a little fossil of some type of plant.

Karin

EVALUATION

Students will be evaluated on

- Participation
- Staying on task
- Using resource materials effectively

Figure 6.16

Seashell

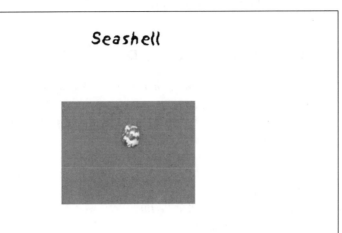

First Draft

This shell is very small. It also looks very cool because of the way the colors are. The other thing is it looks like it has not been polished or anything. It does because the texture is rough and scaly feeling. Then, some people say that you can hear the ocean through a shell. Well, you cannot hear anything through this rock. That is the description of my shell.

Final Copy

This shell is very small, about 2 cm long from the spiral to the end of the tip. It also looks very cool because of the way the colors are. The shell is a brownish black with stripes of white on it. It also has a yellowish color with a little bit of brownish black at the spiral on the top, not very big. The other thing is it looks like it has not been polished or anything. It looks like that because the texture is scaly and it does not feel very smooth, but it is not rough either. Some people say that you can hear the ocean through a shell. Well, you cannot hear anything through this shell.

Rebecca

The final project will be evaluated for

- Completeness (Does the project answer the assigned question?)
- Were resources cited correctly?
- Does the final writing piece distinguish the object from the other objects through the use of adjectives and vivid description?

- Is the information collected accurate?
- Is spelling and punctuation correct?

SUGGESTED READINGS AND RESOURCES

Abbott, R. T. (1985). *Seashells of the world: A guide to the better-known species.* Madison, WI: Turtleback.

Abbott, R. T. (1986). *Seashells of North America: A guide to field identification* (Rev. ed.). New York: Golden.

Gabbi, Giorgio (2000). *Shells: Guide to jewels of the sea.* New York: Abbeville.

Shell collecting. Retrieved May 2002, from http://manandmollusc.net/links_collecting.html

Wonderful world of seashell collecting. Retrieved May 2002, from http://www.seashell-collector.com

Wye, K. W. (1998). *The encyclopedia of shells.* New York: Knickerbocker.

VOCABULARY

adaptations: the characteristics something has that help it survive or adapt to the environment

distinguishing characteristics: the characteristics of an object that make it unique and different from other beings

ACADEMIC STANDARDS

Grade Level: 3–8

National Language Standards

Gathers and uses information for research purposes (ENG. K–12.3)

Uses reading skills and strategies to understand and interpret a variety of information texts (ENG. K–2.3)

Uses listening and speaking strategies for different purposes (ENG. K–12.8)

National Science Standards

Knows that investigations involve systematic observations, carefully collected, relevant evidence, logical reasoning and some imagination in developing hypotheses and explanations (NS.5–8.1 Science as Inquiry)

Understands that questioning and open communications are integral to the process of science (NS.5–8.1 Science as Inquiry)

Knows that organisms have a great variety of body plans and internal structures that serve specific functions for survival (NS5–8.3 Life Science)

WHAT'S YOUR FANTASY?

ESSENTIAL UNDERSTANDING

Big Idea: Fantasy Genre

Essential Understanding(s): Genres have specific characteristics which distinguish them from each other.

OBJECTIVES

Students will

- Identify examples of the fantasy genre found in a video.
- Categorize these fantasy examples into groups based on characteristics.
- Identify the elements of the genre of fantasy by labeling these groups.

MATERIALS

For this lesson you will need

- Video "The Snowman" (Briggs & Raymond, *The Snowman*, Columbia Tri-Star Home Video)
- Video viewing sheet for students (Figure 6.19)
- Chart paper
- Markers

TIME REQUIRED

- Part One (video and recording): forty-five minutes
- Part Two (group recording, categorization, labeling): two to three forty-five-minute sessions

PROCEDURE

1. Give students an opportunity to orally share their definitions of fantasy. Typically you will get examples rather than characteristics that

Figure 6.17   Sources for Objects: Video

In this lesson, the video serves as the "object." I use the video "The Snowman" because it is a wordless video and students can focus on the images. Other videos that are good examples of their genres include:

Cooper, J. F. *The Last of the Mohicans*—historical fiction (Family Home Entertainment)

Paulson, Gary. *A Cry in the Wild*—adventure (MGM/UA Home Video)

Wells, H. G. *The Time Machine*—science fiction (MGM/UA Home Video)

While many people may not see the value of watching video, focused viewing is a skill to be taught, and students are given a great deal of direction in what to look for while they are watching. This medium is one with which students are *very* familiar and in which they will be able to pick out enough good examples to allow this lesson to flow very well. Additionally, this is just the first step in a genre study. They *will* read and write examples from the genre!

Figure 6.18   Fantasy Misconception

At this point, depending on the grade level you teach, you will probably get many examples that are more characteristic of science fiction than fantasy—*lots* of aliens from distant galaxies, two-headed space creatures, and so forth. Other students will be more on the right track with their examples, yet even these students may not have the vocabulary to identify characteristics of the genre. Examples will be more likely than characteristics or definitions.

make up the genre. Do not comment at this point about whether the examples provided are appropriate for the genre; simply let students share.

2.   Provide students with a recording sheet on which to write down ideas as they view the video (Figure 6.19). Tell them that as they watch they should look for all of the examples that they believe are characteristic of fantasy. They should record these examples in the appropriate box on their sheet.

3.   Play the movie and monitor to ensure that all students are attending to the video and remembering to record information about the fantasy characteristics they see.

Figure 6.19 Video Viewing Sheet

In the first box below, record all of the examples of fantasy that you see as you watch the movie, *The Snowman.* Anything that seems like fantasy to you should be written down in the box to share with the class at the conclusion of the video.

In the box below, write the class list of fantasy genre characteristics as we develop them together on the board/chart paper.

4. The second phase of this lesson begins by having students share their ideas from viewing the video. Record *all* of their responses on big pieces of chart paper. Using long sheets of bulletin board paper works even better. This can also be done on the chalkboard but the lesson usually requires more than one session, and it is easier to record student responses on paper that can be rolled up and saved until the next day. Don't worry if a student gives an example that may not quite fit with the definition of fantasy. Just because something is on the paper doesn't mean that it will make it into the final categorization system. Typically "inappropriate" responses will not end up being used. The important thing is to have everyone contribute to the overall class brainstorm list.

5. Once students have given all of the examples from the movie that they have written down on their brainstorm lists, ask the students to take a few minutes to silently review all of the information on the chart paper. Provide several minutes for this and really encourage the students to read carefully and get a feel for the list.

6. Ask students to look over the list again and think about how they would group some of the items because they are alike in some way. In order for the students to come up with the categorization system themselves, it is important that this is the extent of the directions you provide. When a student comes up with a grouping, ask that student for a rationale. Why did they feel that those particular examples should be grouped together? Circle all of the "like" items in the same color marker. Then ask the class for another grouping, again asking for rationale and circling items in another color marker. Continue this process until all related items have been grouped together. Some of the examples will not be used, and this is alright. As stated before, typically these will be the items that were only marginally related to a definition of fantasy.

7. Once all "useable" items have been grouped, students will begin the process of labeling the groups. Ask the class to look at all of the examples circled in a particular color and to figure out a way of defining what they all have in common in general language. This may seem similar to the rationale provided in the last step, but it is actually taking specifics and making them more general and, therefore, applicable to any fantasy text. For example,

- As a rationale, a student may group several things together because in all of them the snowman does things that only humans can do.

- In the group definition stage, this could be defined as, "Inanimate objects take on human qualities." (which you could then define for them as personification).

Figure 6.20

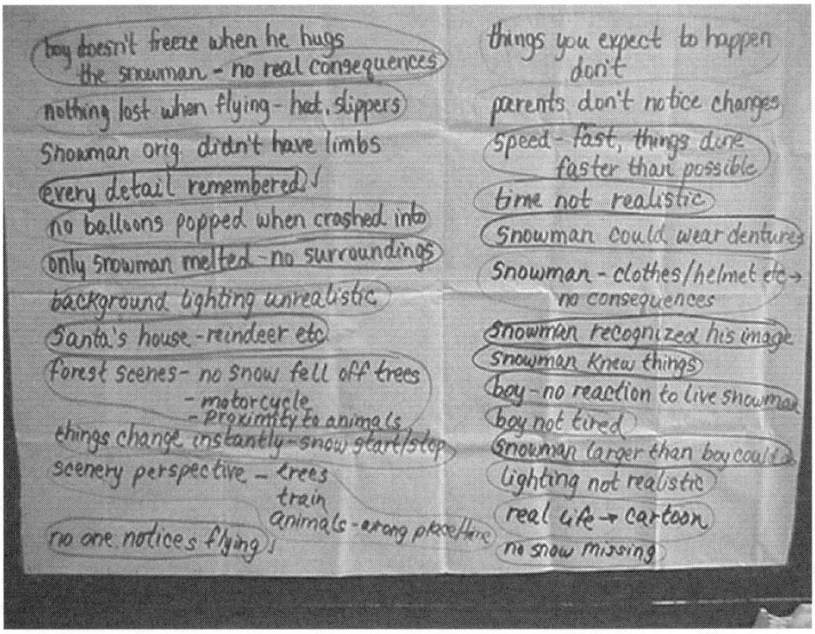

Figure 6.21

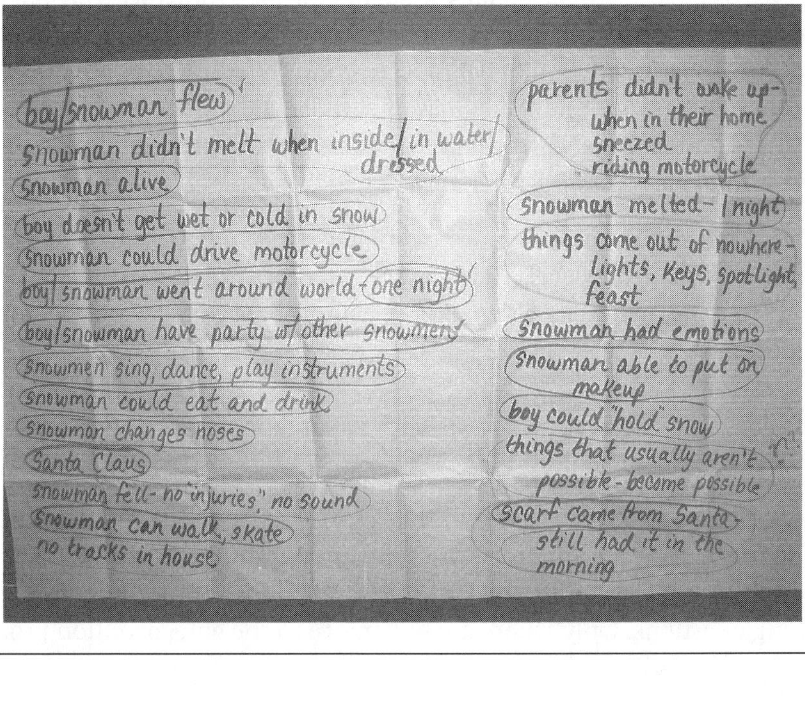

Figure 6.22   Fantasy Characteristics (Defined by a Sixth-Grade Language Arts Class)

People can do things they can't normally do.

Inanimate objects come to life and can do human things.

Things that should happen in real life don't happen.

Passage of time is unrealistic.

Things appear out of nowhere just when they're needed.

Imaginary characters and places exist in the story.

There are no realistic consequences for actions.

Surroundings are fanciful.

8. Continue this process until all groupings have been labeled with general "definitions." These then become the identifying characteristics of the genre. Typically students will identify every one of the major characteristics on their own, and they will have written it in their own language, which is much more understandable to them. Figure 6.22 shows the characteristics of fantasy as defined by a group of sixth graders.

ADAPTATIONS

• For older or higher-ability students (or for groups with whom you have done a great number of categorization/classification lessons), the process of identifying and labeling the groups of examples could be done first in small groups and then shared with the class. Commonalities could be shared and differences could be discussed in the process of coming up with a final class list of genre characteristics.

• Choose the fantasy genre characteristics that are the most appropriate for your grade level. Younger grade levels may only use a few of the characteristics whereas older grades will probably use a more complex definition.

DISCUSSION QUESTIONS

The types of questions needed in this lesson are those that encourage the students to provide rationales for their thinking. Allow students to create the initial brainstorm list of fantasy examples without commenting or asking questions. Only when students move to the categorization process do you want to question their thinking and ask for extensions of their reasoning.

When beginning this process, ask students, "Which items can be grouped together because they are alike in some way?" Notice that this asks " . . . in *some* way" meaning that there is no one correct way to group the examples. It may be necessary at first to tell your students this repeatedly. (And they still won't believe you!)

As students provide a possible grouping of examples, ask them questions such as

- In what way(s) did you feel that these items were alike?

- What did you see that tied these examples together?

Once students have completed the groupings, you will be ready for them to label the groups with general definitions for characteristics of the fantasy genre. Get them started on this process by asking them questions such as

- Look at the (red) group. What do these elements have in common? (Typically you will get something specific to the movie they just watched.)

- How can we take that common characteristic and write it in general words so that it would apply to all fantasy texts?

ASSESSMENT AND EVALUATION

- You can informally assess students' thinking and categorization skills by observing how students think through their rationales for why some examples should be grouped together. This is particularly applicable if you have small student groups work through a categorization system prior to sharing them as a whole class. Alternatively, you could have each individual student identify one grouping and write out a rationale to turn in to you.

- You can collect the students' informal brainstorm list of fantasy examples from their viewing of the video. This can then be used as a baseline to see how students are thinking about the elements of the genre.

- Typically, to ensure that students understand the genre elements they have labeled and defined, I have them analyze several picture books according to their class characteristics list. I put together several book boxes containing a variety of picture books—some fantasy and some not.

Figure 6.23   Student Work Sample

Characteristic	Yes/No	Example(s) from Story
People can do things they can't normally do.	Yes	The boy went to the North Pole by train and met Santa.
Personification is evident.	No	
Things that should happen in real life don't happen.	Yes	His parents don't wake up from the noise of the train.
Passage of time is unrealistic.	Yes	The boy went all the way to the North Pole and back and still had time to sleep.
Things appear out of nowhere just when they're needed.	Yes	The train appears in front of the boy's house.
Imaginary characters and places exist in the story.	Yes	Santa Claus and the reindeer are at the workshop at the North Pole.
There are no realistic consequences for actions.	Yes	The boy doesn't get cold.
Surroundings are unrealistic.	Yes	All of the North Pole looked just as all of the fairy tales say.

I usually have a small group read through the books in a box together and decide which ones are fantasies and which are not, justifying their decisions by using the characteristics list. On another day, I have the groups take out a different book box, and each individual in the group takes one picture book and does the analysis individually.

• You could also have students write fantasy stories that include a specific number of the genre characteristics identified.

EXTENSIONS AND MODIFICATIONS

Extend the categorization process by asking students to engage in the process twice. Make a second set of chart papers listing all of the examples

Figure 6.24   Student Work Sample

Characteristic	Yes/No	Example(s) from Story
People can do things they can't normally do.	Yes	People went to the North Pole to meet Santa Claus.
Personification is evident.	No	
Things that should happen in real life don't happen.	Yes	Only people who believed in Santa Claus could hear the bell.
Passage of time is unrealistic.	Yes	The boy went to the North Pole in one night.
Things appear out of nowhere just when they're needed.	Yes	The train came on no tracks. The bell appeared at the end.
Imaginary characters and places exist in the story.	Yes	Elves Santa Claus Flying reindeer
There are no realistic consequences for actions.	No	
Surroundings are unrealistic.	Yes	There is a fancy city at the North Pole.

and have it ready. Once the students have grouped all of the examples and given rationales, take those chart papers down and put up the second set. Repeat the process asking students to come up with a completely different way of grouping the examples. As a class, choose the list they want to use in developing the characteristic list.

SUGGESTED READINGS AND RESOURCES

Buss, K. & Karnowski, L. (2000). *Reading and Writing Literary Genres.* Newark, DE: International Reading Association.

Cunningham, J. G. (Ed.). (2002). *Science fiction.* San Diego, CA: Greenhaven.

Mass, W. & Levine, S. P. (Eds.). (2002). *Fantasy.* San Diego, CA: Greenhaven.

McCarthy, T. (1996) Historical fiction. In *Teaching genre—Grades 4–8*. New York: Scholastic Professional Development.

McCarthy, T. (1996) Science fiction. In *Teaching genre—Grades 4–8*. New York: Scholastic Professional Development.

VOCABULARY

genre: a particular style of literature with specific characteristics

fantasy: a genre of literature with fanciful characteristics (see Figure 6.22).

ACADEMIC STANDARDS

Grade Level: 4–8

Language:

Analyzing a film (and picture books) for particular characteristics (ENG.K–12.3 Evaluation Strategies)

Discuss similarities between literary features of the "text"(video) (ENG.K–12.6 Applying Knowledge)

Categorize information and label categories based on group similarities

Develop a definition for a specific genre of literature through inquiry and categorization

Science Lesson Plans 7

- ➢ ZONE HOME
- ➢ BIRDS OF A FEATHER
- ➢ WHOSE TRACK IS THAT?
- ➢ SCIENCE ROCKS

ZONE HOME

ESSENTIAL UNDERSTANDING

Big Idea: Adaptation

Essential Understanding(s): Environmental characteristics lead to adaptation aids in survival.

OBJECTIVES

Students will

- Observe characteristics of a marine organism
- Use observations to generate guiding research questions
- Research in order to gain enough information to hypothesize about the characteristics of a marine organism's environment
- Classify marine organisms
- Determine environmental characteristics of ocean zones either through use of research information or through prediction
- Hypothesize adaptations of successful marine organisms in each zone

MATERIALS

For this lesson you will need

- A variety of marine specimens
- Hand lenses
- Drawing paper and pencils
- Resource/research material selected to meet reading needs in your class
- Chalk board/white board/chart paper; chalk or pens

Figure 7.1   Sources for Objects: Marine Organisms

Most of the marine organisms I use for this lesson came from dollar stores at the beach. You can find a wide variety of shells and organisms such as starfish, horseshoe crabs, sponges, and coral. Most of the organisms are very inexpensive—many less than a dollar. I have even found nautilus and sea-horses, although they are a little more expensive to purchase. Other specimens such as squid, octopus, shrimp, and fish can be purchased whole from your grocer and stored in alcohol and water in mason jars.

TIME REQUIRED

- Specimen observation, question development: approximately forty-five minutes

- Research varies, typically one to two hours

- Categorization/grouping of organisms and zone identification: forty-five minutes to one hour

PROCEDURE

1. Present students with the basic problem which you would like their help in solving. Any story scenario will work; I use something like the following:

> *This summer a group of us went out on an expedition to collect marine specimens for our school system's collection of natural objects. We went to the same location, but we were then split into two groups based on how far down in the ocean we would be going to collect the specimens. One group stayed relatively close to the surface while the second group went farther down. Once we returned to the research lab on shore, we discovered that the specimen collections were quite different. We were so excited about our discoveries and sent them back to the school division's science department. Unfortunately, we forgot to tell the people here that the specimens needed to be kept in their two separate groups so that they could be studied. When the specimens arrived, they were unpacked and put all together into one big collection. We need your help today to determine which specimens belong in which group. By the end of our work time, we need all of the specimens separated into their original groups.*

2. After presenting students with the problem, give each table a tray containing varied marine organisms on it and ask them to observe them and then to choose one that they would like to investigate. I try to have more specimens on the tray than students in the group so that all students feel they have a choice.

3. All students should choose one specimen and examine it carefully with the following questions in mind: *What is your organism? Where in the ocean would you find this organism living?* I ask students to think about what features of the organism might help them to answer those questions. I then ask students to develop "sub-questions" that would help them answer those larger questions. I also ask students to draw their specimen, paying careful attention to details.

4. After students have had time to develop their own questions, I ask them to share their questions with those at their table, adding new questions that others give that they hadn't thought of themselves. I repeat this process with the whole class sharing aloud. In this way, all students can develop questions and can benefit from hearing others' as well. I list all of their questions on the board.

5. Students then use their own questions to guide their research. I provide numerous reference and nonfiction books to help them answer their questions. I make sure students realize that while they don't have to answer every question on the board, they do have to answer enough of them to be able to hypothesize into which group the organism should be placed. This part of the lesson can take as long as you'd like it to take— from one class period to several days.

6. Once students feel that they have enough information to make an informed hypothesis, I have students share their findings. I record details about the environment on the board or on chart paper. (These details are given to me by the students as they share their research.) Students who feel that their organisms also belong in that environment can add to that information. Students who believe that their organisms belong in the second group can tell me to start a second category of descriptors. We continue until all students have shared and thus all organisms are grouped. All students must provide a rationale for why they believe their organism belongs in a particular group; this rationale must be based on their research findings.

7. We read through the first list of environmental characteristics together and hypothesize about the name of that environment. Usually students figure out that the top zone is the Light Zone. We do the same for the second group, the Twilight Zone. At this point in the lesson students have figured out the names of the first two zones of the ocean, the characteristics of those zones, and the characteristics of the organisms which inhabit those zones.

8. Since there are very few organisms available from the bottom zone (Midnight Zone), we predict the zone characteristics and organism adaptations by referring to what we know about the first two zones. Then I typically have students create their own Midnight Zone organism, the only requirement being that it have authentic adaptations to allow it to live in that zone. Model Magic works really well for this activity as students can form it into any shape they need. I then have them write descriptive paragraphs about their organism, explaining why it has particular adaptations.

Figure 7.2

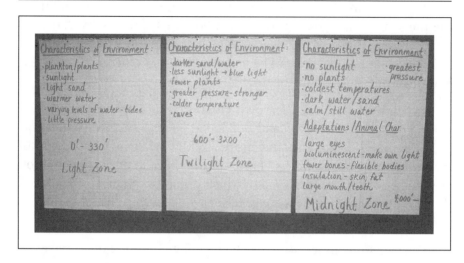

ADAPTATIONS

The level of reading material provided is an easy way to adapt this lesson to meet the needs of your class. There are a wide variety of nonfiction/ reference books available at all reading levels.

This lesson also lends itself to connections with many other subject areas. Once students have made predictions as a class about the physical characteristics of the Midnight Zone and the adaptations of the animals who live there, they can design an animal who would live there and write a paragraph describing its adaptations and features. These creatures can be designed and described in groups or individually depending on the ability level of your class. There are numerous graphic organizers that can be used to help students with less writing ability or experience plan out a cause/effect paragraph (environmental characteristic → adaptation).

DISCUSSION QUESTIONS

Although you want the majority of the questions to come from the students, you will begin the lesson by providing an overarching question for them to work from: What is this animal and where would you find it in the ocean?

Your job as the teacher will be to facilitate the development of research questions through your own carefully worded questions. For example, when students ask about a specific feature on their organism, you might ask them to hypothesize about its function.

The main point at which your questions will be key will be in the grouping phase. Students should always be asked to provide a rationale for their choices. Remember that the *process* that students use to arrive at a decision

Figure 7.3   Sample Student Report

Bug-Eyed Fish

This is a bug-eyed fish. My fish lives in the Midnight Zone. He has bug-eyes so he can see in the dark water. He has razor-sharp teeth to catch his prey. He has a bioluminescent light that hangs over his head like a lantern so he can light his way across the dark water. His coloration is dark so he can camouflage from his predators. He has a flexible body and very few bones so he can handle the great amount of pressure that is down there. He also has very thick skin and insulation to keep him warm in the freezing cold water. I think this animal should be real. He has all the characteristics of an animal that really lives way down there in the Midnight Zone.

about how to group their organism is just as important (if not more!) as grouping it "correctly." (After all, few organisms "stay put" in one zone at all times). Questions such as, "What made you think . . . ?" or "What part of your research guided you to think . . ." are appropriate here. You will most likely find that the other students will also ask questions if they perceive that another student is "off-track." I once had a student who initially placed his organism in the lower zone because it hid behind rocks. But then he indicated that it also ate plants. Another student pointed out that plants couldn't live in the lower depths because there is no light. This gave me a chance to then address the idea that there is a "bottom" to every zone where rocks would exist and not just one bottom to the ocean, a common misconception among elementary students.

EVALUATION

Informal assessment of students' research skills can be done while circulating among the students to facilitate their research.

It is most important in this lesson that students be evaluated in terms of their thinking processes. It is more important to hear what they have to say and the conclusions they draw as a result of their research than that they correctly classify their organism. Of course, their grouping needs to be tied logically to their research, and this can be easily assessed through their oral explanation.

Another point for formal evaluation can come in the creation of their Midnight Zone creatures and the descriptive paragraphs that accompany them. Not only can you assess writing skills and the use of appropriate cause and effect key words, but in terms of science, you can also ascertain whether students are understanding the connections between the physical characteristics of an environment and the accompanying adaptations.

EXTENSIONS

Another option here is to turn the Midnight Zone product into a "matching game." Put the animal models out on a table and tape the descriptive paragraphs up on the wall. See if other students can pick out the creature being described in the paragraph.

SUGGESTED READINGS AND RESOURCES

Bittinger, G. (1993). *Exploring water and the ocean.* Everett, WA: Warren.
Khaiwei, Weng, L., & Zheng. *Oceans—Probing the unfathomed depths.* Thinkquest. Retrieved February, 2002, from http://library.thinkquest.org/25471/tzones.htm
Light zones. What's it like where you live—Temperate oceans. Retrieved February, 2002, from http://mbgnet.mobot.org/salt/oceans/zone.htm

VOCABULARY

adaptations: a change in either physical characteristics or behavior to meet environmental conditions

light zone: physical depth of the ocean between approximately 0 and 320 feet, characterized by light, plant life, little pressure, and warmer water

twilight zone: physical depth of the ocean between approximately 600 and 3,200 feet, characterized by dim blue light, higher levels of pressure, and colder water

midnight zone: physical depth of the ocean greater than approximately 4,000 feet, characterized by no light, intense pressure, and freezing water

ACADEMIC STANDARDS

Grade Level: 3–8

Science:

Observing specimens for details (NS.K–4.1 and NS.5–8.1 Science as Inquiry)

Developing and investigating research questions (NS.K–4.1 and NS.5–8.1 Science as Inquiry)

Categorizing animals based on research (NS.K–4.3 and NS.5–8.3 Life Science)

Matching animal characteristics to environmental characteristics (NS.K–4.3 and NS.5–8.3 Life Science)

Predicting animal adaptations based on environmental characteristics (NS.5–8.3 Life Science)

Predicting environmental characteristics of an unknown (NS.K–4.3 and NS.5–8.3 Life Science)

Predicting animal adaptations based on environmental characteristics (NS.K–4.3 and NS.5–8.3 Life Science)

Social Studies

Researching characteristics and spatial distribution of ecosystems on Earth (NS.K–4.3 and NS.5–8.3 Life Science)

Language

Research information about marine organisms (ENG.K–12.7 Evaluating Data and ENG.K–12.8 Developing Research Skills)

Share information orally including rationale for categorization (ENG.K–12.4 Communication skills

Write descriptive paragraphs describing Midnight Zone creatures (ENG.K–12.5 Communication Strategies)

BIRDS OF A FEATHER

ESSENTIAL UNDERSTANDING

Big Idea: Investigation

Essential Understanding: Observing the distinguishing characteristics of a feather can lead to the discovery that all animals in the same class do not have the same characteristics but are distinctly different and adapt to the needs they have to obtain food.

OBJECTIVES

Students will

- Collect, record, and report data.
- Make accurate measurements using basic tools.
- Understand that organisms have distinguishing characteristics.
- Understand that an organism's body adapts to its niche.

MATERIALS

For this lesson you will need

- Birds of a Feather worksheet, found at end of lesson
- A collection of feathers from different kinds of birds, including nocturnal birds and waterfowl, or pictures of feathers
- Gram scale (if using actual feathers)
- Rulers with centimeters
- Resource materials to help students discover the kind of bird their feather comes from
- Magnifying glasses

TIME REQUIRED

This lesson takes about a week of fifty-minute periods to complete. The first class period is used for observing, measuring, predicting and writing about the feather, along with sharing the observations and predictions with the class. The next few class periods are used for research and verification of the students' findings. Remember, it is not as important that the students' answers are correct as it is that they make sense.

Figure 7.4   Sources for Objects: Feathers

This is a collection that needs to be started long before this lesson is implemented. I use feathers I have collected over a period of time, thanks to my cats and other teachers in our county who have heard of the collection. It is possible to collect feathers from different craft stores and then do the research yourself to find out what birds they are from and what geographic area the birds are found in. If you find you are not comfortable using real feathers, then pictures of feathers will work as well, although you will have to delete the weighing and the measuring of the feathers. Also it is a great thrill for students to work with real feathers. Not often do students get to touch, feel, or handle a real feather.

PROCEDURE

1. Group students into pairs.

2. Place appropriate measuring tools and resource books in a central area.

3. Hand out a feather from the collection. Although I usually store them in plastic bags, I encourage the students to remove them for measurement and closer observation with a magnifying glass. Tell the students what geographic region the feathers came from.

4. Working in pairs, students will make observations about their feather. They will record their observations on the worksheet. If using real

Figure 7.5

Birds of a Feather

To find out more about the bird your feather may have come from make the following observations:

1. weight   _____

2. length   _____

3. width at widest point   _____

4. color(s)   _____

Using complete sentences, predict what kind of bird your feather came from. Include **three** reasons why you think it came from that bird.

Prediction: _____

_____

_____

_____

_____

Prepare to present your findings and your predictions to the class.

Now, list 10 questions you would like answered about your feather or the bird it came from.

1.   _____

2.   _____

3.   _____

4.   _____

5.   _____

6.   _____

7.   _____

8.   _____

9.   _____

10.   _____

Now research your feather. Try to find out what bird the feather came from. Back up your answer with facts you have found about the bird. Be ready to report to the class about your findings and your justifications.

feathers, the students should weigh and measure the length and width at different points of the feather. They should look closely at the shaft of the feather and the fringe. They will make a prediction as to what kind of bird their feather came from and give three reasons why they think so. Then they will generate a list of questions they have about either the bird the feather came from or the feather itself. I do not allow one of the questions to be "what bird did this feather come from?" since that is what they are trying to discover.

5.   Students will present their findings to the class. The class will ask questions related to their findings to help them with the next step.

6.   Based on their predictions, students will begin research to verify their predictions. They will change their predictions as they find research to back them up.

7.   Students will prepare a written and oral report of their findings. Since you are not looking for a correct answer, as much as one that makes sense, the reports should include information that backs up their prediction. They will create visual support for their report in the form of a poster.

8.   Students will share their discovery process with the class and their findings through the oral report.

DISCUSSION QUESTIONS

This lesson will test the patience of your students. Many begin this lesson thinking that all feathers are alike, and the idea that they aren't can be a little overwhelming at times. In this lesson, students want to know if they are correct. Emphasizing the research process and the sensibility of their answer is a way to keep them going, without giving away the answer, thus stopping the research process. Rather than answering them directly, you can guide their research through the following questions:

- Does the bird you predict the feather came from live in the correct geographic region?
- Are all feathers on a bird alike?
- What part of the bird do you think your feather came from?
- Is your prediction reasonable? Does the size of the feather fit the size of the bird? Is it too large or too small?

• What does the feather tell you about the habits of the bird? How is your feather different from the other feathers? Why might they be different?

ASSESSMENT AND EVALUATION

Informally, students will be evaluated on

- Participation
- Staying on task
- Using resource materials effectively

A formal evaluation will be taken on the final project including

• Accuracy. Although the answer does not have to be entirely accurate, it should be reasonable. A guess of "penguin" in the case of a feather from a bird living in the northeast would not be reasonable. A guess of a "hummingbird" from a feather eight centimeters long would also not be a reasonable answer.

• Distinguishing characteristics of the bird researched. Final reports should include a description of the bird they think the feather is from. The report should include how those characteristics help the bird survive in its environment. Where the feather came from on the bird should be a part of the report. Students should justify their answer through the research they have completed (see Figure 7.6).

• A poster. Created for the oral presentation to the class, it will include a picture of the feather, the written report, and a picture of the bird.

EXTENSIONS AND MODIFICATIONS

• This activity can be done in the same manner using bird nests. When using bird nests, other indicators about the builder of the nest can be what materials the nest is made from, where the nest may have been found, the size of the nest in relation to the size of the bird, and so on.

• The feather activity could be followed up using bird nests. Students who finish quickly can be given a bird nest and told to follow the same process.

Figure 7.6   Sample Student Reports

The Turkey Vulture

We figured out that our feather came from a turkey vulture. The vulture's feathers are used as camouflage, with a lighter color on the bottom of the wing instead of having darker color on top. The normal length of a larger feather is around 35 centimeters. The vulture's feathers have a protruding group of vanes to help them glide much easier. If the vanes were spread apart like down, the bird would not be able to fly well. Down feathers are mostly used for insulation or warmth.

Turkey vultures have no feathers around their neck like we thought they did. They also have long, curved feathers for great flight and gliding. Their average size is about 27 inches, but they can grow up to 31 inches. Vultures eat mostly dead organisms or scavenge for other scraps of food. The bird has a long, white, very sharp beak. Its talons are not very sharp, making it unable to grasp dead carcasses. Finally, turkey vultures have a great immune system and rarely get sick.

Ring Necked Pheasant

Our feather is from the Ring Necked Pheasant. Before we knew it was the Ring Necked Pheasant, we guessed it was from a goose. We found out that it wasn't a goose because when we looked up the goose, we realized the feather didn't fit the goose at all. The colors and size were totally different. The feathers of the Ring Necked Pheasant are there for camouflage in the grasses and leaves. There are many different colored feathers on the bird, and many different sized feathers, but our feather is one of the longest found on the bird. The longest feather comes from the tail. This feather came from the wing.

The Ring Necked Pheasant lives in grassy areas in the northeast portion of the United States They nest in the high grasses where predators can't see them. They lay six to ten buff-colored eggs. The nesting period is at its peak from May to July.

The pheasant eats seeds of corn, wheat, oats, foxtail, ragweed, grapes, poison ivy, bittersweet sumac, and dogweed. They feed the babies berries and insects.

The adult male pheasants weight 1.8 to 3.5 pounds. The adult female weigh from 1.6 to 2.2 pounds. The length of an adult is from 33 to 36 inches, for a male, and 20 to 22 inches for a female. Their tails can get up to 21 inches long, for a male. This bird doesn't shed its feathers.

The sizes of the feathers do affect how it flies. The feathers are heavy and the wings are small. This bird can only fly a short distance before getting tired. That is how its predator, the fox, usually get the pheasant. It is a hard life for the Ring Necked Pheasant, and they only live a few years before dying.

• The feather activity could be followed up with a study of bird beaks and how bird beaks have adapted for the gathering of food or nest-building in their habitat.

SUGGESTED READINGS AND RESOURCES

eNature. *Nature and wildlife field guides.* Retrieved June, 2002, from http://www. enature.com/guides/select_Birds.asp

Kitchen, B. (1993). *And so they build.* Cambridge, MA: Candlewick.

Koch, M. J. (1998). *Bird, egg, feather, nest.* New York: Smithmark.

Peterson, R. T. (1990). *A field guide to birds.* Boston: Houghton Mifflin.

Zim, H. S. & Gabrielson, I. N. (1987). *Birds.* New York: Golden.

VOCABULARY

shaft: the part of the feather in the middle that holds the fringe

inner vane, outer vane: the part of the feather that faces away from the wind, and the part that faces into the wind

fringe: the part of the feather at the top that breaks up the flow of air and silences the flight

ACADEMIC STANDARDS

Grade Level: 3–8

National Science Standards

> Knows that investigations involve systematic observations, carefully collected, relevant evidence, logical reasoning, and some imagination in developing hypothesis and explanations (NS.5–8.1 Science as Inquiry)

> Understands that questioning and open communication are integral to the process of science (NS.5–8.1 Science as Inquiry)

> Uses appropriate tools and techniques to gather, analyze, and interpret scientific data (NS.5–8.1 Science as Inquiry)

> Knows that organisms have a great variety of body plans and internal structures that serve specific functions for survival (NS.5–8.3 Life Science)

National Language Standards:

Gathers and uses information for research purposes (ENG.K–12.3)

Uses reading skills and strategies to understand and interpret a variety of information texts (ENG.K–12.3)

Uses listening and speaking strategies for different purposes (ENG.K–12.8)

WHOSE TRACK IS THAT?

ESSENTIAL UNDERSTANDING

Big Idea: Animal tracks tell a story.

Essential Understanding: Information about an animal and its adaptations can be gained through close observation of an animal track.

OBJECTIVES

Students will

- Determine the characteristics of an animal by the track it leaves behind.
- Collect, record, and report data.
- Make accurate measurements using basic tools.
- Know that scientific investigation involves asking and answering questions and comparing the answers to what scientists already know.

MATERIALS

For this lesson you will need:

- Pictures of different animal tracks (available at *http://www. humboldt.net/~tracker/index.html* or
- Molds for creating animal tracks available through science supply companies or your art teacher
- Field guides for mammals
- An animal track measuring chart to help identify the track by size and position
- Crayons, markers, or colored pencils
- Drawing paper
- Resource materials to help students discover information about the animal that made the track, beyond what the track can tell them
- Ink, acrylic paint, or tempera paint
- Soft, plastic-based clay
- Small sheet or piece of muslin or bulletin board paper (optional for extension activity)

Figure 7.7   Sources for Objects: Animal Tracks

> You have a few different sources for objects for this lesson. I was lucky enough to have the art teacher purchase a set of animal molds for our school. We found them in a science supply catalog. There were a variety of tracks and a wide span in prices, ranging from $45.00 a set to much higher. The students were able to make tracks in clay, cover them with paint, and create a story using the prints. If you are on a limited budget, you can also download tracks on the Internet. Some good websites for tracks and information can be found in the resource section.

TIME REQUIREMENTS

Investigating and observing the tracks, along with making the prints, takes from forty-five minutes to an hour, depending on the age of the students. Taking accurate measurements is critical to finding out the owner of the track and should be emphasized. After making predictions and writing up a paragraph that includes all their information, students need time to investigate the animal they predict it might be. I found that using the Internet sites that include field guides makes this an easier task. It also takes about an hour. Planning out a story, writing it up, and making a story map takes about forty-five minutes.

PROCEDURE

1.   Ask the students what they think finding an animal track can tell them about an animal. List their ideas on chart paper or on the blackboard.

2.   Place students in small groups or pairs. Tell students they are going to investigate the front and back track of an unknown animal. Give them the casts that you have already made from the molds with the names scratched out or give them pictures of tracks without the name of the animal.

3.   Ask them to investigate their casts and make observations about the track. Have them press the tracks into the soft clay to make a realistic track, as if in mud. Encourage them to walk around and look at other students' tracks for comparison. Have the students make a list of their observations about their tracks.

4.   Students should predict the size of their animal, where it makes its home (burrow, tree, etc.), what it eats, about how much it weighs, and what kind of animal it is. They should back up their predictions with reasons why they have chosen that animal. They should generate a list of questions they need to research in order to verify their prediction.

Figure 7.8

Animal Tracks

Front Track	Hind Track
Small claws	No claws
Bumpy texture	Rough
3.5 cm long	4 cm long
5 toes	5 toes
Big creases	Small creases
Rough	Toes 1 cm apart
Fur marks	Fur marks

We think our animal is the raccoon. Its claws always stick out so it can climb trees, dig holes for bugs and get into garbage. The front claws are for hanging onto its prey when eating. The hind feet are for keeping its balance when using its front claws for eating.

5. Students will present their findings to the class. The questions generated by each group will be listed on the board, which students may draw upon for the next step.

6. Students will begin research to verify their predictions. They will change their predictions if their research suggests they should. Students should write up their findings in the form of a report that will be presented to the class.

7. When the students believe they have verified their predictions or found out what their animal is, a list of the animals should be made on the board.

8. Have students experiment with different kinds of ink or paint to produce a footprint using the tracks. They should create a good print, spacing the front and back feet the correct distance apart.

9. Students will display their footprints and their reports to the class. They can also be asked to create a food web using all the animal tracks displayed in the class. They can then create a picture story using the different tracks.

Figure 7.9   Sample Student Report

Black-Tailed Jackrabbits

Black-tailed jackrabbits depend on their feet for many things. The hind foot is much larger than the front foot. When the jackrabbit hops, its hind feet jump in front of the front feet and push off for more power. At their top speed, jackrabbits can leap 20 feet. Normally they tend to hop 5 to 10 feet.

Figure 7.10   Sample Student Report

Footprint Report by Rebecca, Amy, and Micca

We think that the animal is a beaver. The hind feet are webbed like a beaver and the front feet have claws. The feet also have fur, which is used to protect the animal. We think that the hind feet are used for walking on hard surfaces. Our prediction is that the front feet are used for climbing and for swimming and those are the reasons why the hind and front feet are different. The depth of the front foot is ½ cm. And the hind is 3 cm. Both feet have 5 toes, which are 2 to 3 centimeters apart. The length of the hind foot is 14.5 cm. long and 3.5 cm. wide. Our group hopes to learn more about the beaver.

Questions:

1. What animal does the beaver prey upon?

2. What animals are the beaver's predators?

3. Why does the beaver live in water and on land?

4. Where does the beaver prefer to live?

5. How does the beaver defend itself?

6. Why do beavers build dams?

DISCUSSION QUESTIONS

1. Does the distance between the front and back track tell you anything about the size of the animal?

2. Do the tracks animals leave behind always show both the front and back feet?

3. Does the thickness of the padding tell you anything about the animal? Does the spacing of the pads tell you anything about the animal? Does it tell you anything about the environment it lives in?

Figure 7.11 Predator-Prey Track Story

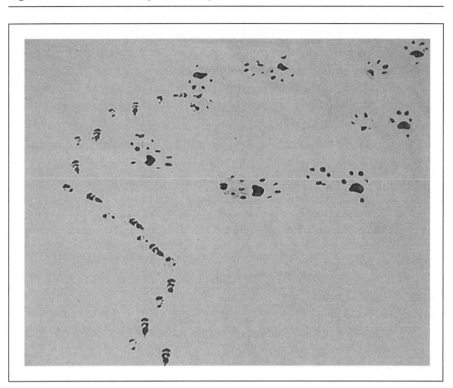

4. Does the presence of claws or the lack of claws tell you anything about the animal?

5. Can animal tracks tell you anything about the speed of the animal?

EVALUATION

The individual students will be formally evaluated for

- Neatness of their footprints and project
- Accuracy in reproducing footprints
- Oral and written report
- Verification of their answer

EXTENSIONS

Have students create a scenario involving two or more of the animals (perhaps a predator/prey relationship, a food chain, etc.). Have students create that scene on the fabric using acrylic paints. Be sure they place the tracks the correct distance apart. The tracks should tell some kind of story about the meeting of more than two animals. Display the track story in the hall, along with a piece of chart paper, and have students who pass by write what they think has happened. (See Figure 7.11.)

Take students on a field trip to an area around the school on the search for animal tracks. Make plaster molds of any tracks you find. Investigate the animal that may have left the track.

Create a muddy area near the playground at the end of the day that is not too wet. Check the next morning for footprints left behind.

Talk about how forensic experts use tracks to help them solve crimes.

SUGGESTED RESOURCES AND READINGS

Animal tracks (Discovery Box). (1996). New York: Scholastic.

Cabrera, K. A. *Animal tracks of Humboldt County.* Retrieved June, 2002, from http://www.humboldt.net/~tracker/index.html

Chase, M. & Nasco, Charles (1969). *Field guide to tracks.* Fort Atkinson, WI: Nasco.

eNature. *Nature and wildlife field guides.* Retrieved June, 2002, from http://www.enature.com/guides/select_Birds.asp

Selsam, M. E. (1999). *Big tracks, little tracks.* New York: HarperCollins.

ACADEMIC STANDARDS:

Grade Level: 4–8

Science (National Standards)

Plans and conducts simple investigations (NS.3–5.12)

Knows that different people may interpret the same set of observations differently (NS.3–5.12)

Knows that organisms have a great variety of body plans and internal structures that serve specific functions for survival (NS.6–8.5)

Knows that living organisms have distinct structures and body systems (NS.6–8.5)

Math (National Standards)

Formulate questions that can be addressed with data and display relevant data to answer questions (NM-Data.6–8.1)

Develop and evaluate inferences and predictions that are based on data (NM-Data6–8.3)

SCIENCE ROCKS

ESSENTIAL UNDERSTANDING

Big Idea: Change

Essential Understanding(s): Rocks are part of a cycle of change. Rocks are classified according to characteristics they have at a particular point in this change cycle.

OBJECTIVES

Students will

- Observe characteristics of a group of rocks.
- Categorize the rocks according to similarities and differences.
- Create a grouping system and label its components.
- Explain the grouping system, providing a rationale for why certain rocks belong in specific groups.

MATERIALS

For this lesson you will need

- Identical collections of different types of rocks (enough for every small group of students to have fifteen to twenty rocks; the collections should all contain the same types of rock samples)
- Sticky labels
- Recording sheet and pencils

TIME REQUIRED

Allow approximately a week for:

- Small group classification/reclassification: one forty-five-minute class period
- Small group sharing and problem assignment: one forty-five-minute class period

Figure 7.12   Sources for Objects: Rocks

Most nature stores (or even better, rock and mineral stores) have small collections of rocks for sale. These are great because the specific rock name is right there for you—all you have to do is look it up to see what type of rock it is (and sometimes even that information is provided for you!) Additionally, most states have an office or department of geology that provides, if not free rock samples, at least information about where to locate rock samples. This is a great way to tie in state geography if you teach that as well. You can find contact information for your state's geology office on the Internet. Again, these rocks will most often come with labels, which is very helpful. Students are another great source of rocks—of course you'd have to know a little bit more about rocks to correctly identify these donations or at least be able to research to identify the name and rock type.

- Research and display case development: varies depending on grade level and how much time you want to devote to research; typically this can be done in two to three forty-five-minute class periods

PROCEDURE

1. Divide students into small groups and provide each group with a collection of rocks. These collections should be identical for all groups and should contain approximately fifteen to twenty rocks. Be sure that the collection contains samples from each of the three classifications of rocks—sedimentary, igneous, and metamorphic.

2. Tell students that their job is to classify the rocks according to similar characteristics and to prepare to share their rationale for classification with the class. You may choose to give students a specific number of groups to use, or you may choose to allow students to classify the rocks into as many groupings as they find necessary. Have students record their grouping information on a recording sheet, including rock numbers and the distinguishing characteristics used to place rocks into specific groups.

3. It works well to have students work through several different classification systems before deciding on a final one to share. I ask students to carefully record their grouping information for one classification and then to completely redo the classification in a totally different way, again carefully recording the information. Once students have completed three or four different classifications, they have gotten past the more obvious rock characteristics, such as coloration and size, and are beginning to look at

Figure 7.13   Collection Preparation

It is important that the collections used with each small group are identical so that the students can talk about their classification by referring to rocks that the other students are familiar with. Using sticky labels also helps in this regard. When you purchase individual rocks or a rock set, be sure that there are several samples of a particular rock. Apply a sticky label to the rocks and number them all the same. Be sure to keep a key for yourself!

more subtle characteristics such as evidence of bands, size of crystals, conglomeration, and so forth.

4.   Once students have had a chance to work through several groupings of rocks and have recorded their reasoning for each one, they should choose one to share with the class. This sharing works very effectively if the other students also have their rock collections out and can manipulate the rocks into the groups being discussed by one group. Of course, this only works if the collections are identical and are numbered in exactly the same way.

5.   Once all groups have shared, ask all students to gather around their small group collection and reclassify the rocks according to a system you put on the board. Write up the numbers of rocks that belong together because they are sedimentary rocks. Do not provide students with the label "sedimentary" yet, however. Simply tell them that scientists often classify these particular rocks together. Repeat this process for the igneous and metamorphic rocks in the collection.

6.   Tell students that their job is to figure out why scientists would group these particular rocks together. They should examine the rocks for similarities within the group as well as for differences from the other two groups and should try to figure out scientific labels for the three groups. Ultimately, they will need to create a display case providing visitors to the school with information about how scientists classify rocks, characteristics of the three rock types, and how each group of rocks is formed.

7.   I provide a variety of text and Internet resources for students to use throughout this process. Often students will stumble upon a picture of a rock that resembles a sample in their collection, and the accompanying textual information will help them identify the rock as sedimentary, igneous, or metamorphic. From this point they can discover how that type of rock is formed. Frequently this information leads them to make

Figure 7.14   Rock Cycle and Change

Typically through their research students will discover that one type of rock used to be another type of rock or becomes a different rock type when conditions change. This discovery leads naturally to a discussion of the rock cycle and how each group of rocks fits into this change cycle. I usually don't have to bring this up myself–the students take care of this through their research.

predictions about other rocks in the collection based on their appearance (i.e., they will predict sedimentary if the rock appears to be made up of individual particles).

8. At the conclusion of the week, students should have discovered through research the reasons why you grouped the rocks together into the three groups you presented to them. They should have the following information for each grouping:

- Group name used by scientists
- Characteristics of the group
- How the rocks in the group were formed

Students can share their work in a variety of ways, but actually creating the display case for the school is extremely motivating for students. I usually also have students share their results orally with the class.

ADAPTATIONS

- The level of reading/research material will be the most obvious adaptation that will need to be made to meet the needs of your class. The level of explanation found in different levels of books will also determine the level of display text students will be able to put together.

- To change the complexity of the research process, assign each small group of students to only one grouping of rocks. They should focus in on just this group to identify the group name, characteristics, and formation information. Then the groups can share information with the whole class so that everyone has information on all three rock types.

DISCUSSION QUESTIONS

During phase one when small groups are classifying and reclassifying their rock collections, you will mainly be asking students to explain their thinking with questions such as

- What characteristics do these rocks share that caused you to group them together?

- How are these rocks distinct from those found in the other two groupings?

- In what other way(s) might you group these rocks?

As students share what they consider to be their best classification system, you may need to again ask for specific characteristics that caused students to group certain rocks together.

As students examine the reclassified rock collections (sedimentary, igneous, and metamorphic), you may need to guide students toward focusing on more specific details of the rocks using such questions as

- What do you notice about the consistency of the rock?

- What do you notice about the coloration or differences in coloration?

- What does the rock seem to be made up of? Do you recognize anything else within the rock?

Throughout the research/observation time, you may need to help students refine their thinking so that the characteristics they are developing are truly distinguishing characteristics rather than general characteristics that could apply to more than one rock type. You would simply ask students questions such as

- In what way is that characteristic unique to this rock group?

- In what way(s) could another rock group demonstrate the same characteristic?

- Would such a characteristic enable you to distinguish between *all* of the rocks in this group and *all* other rocks in the other two groups?

ASSESSMENT AND EVALUATION

- During the first phase of this lesson, you should be most concerned with students' classifying skills as well as the rationales they can provide for the different classification systems they develop in their small groups. It is not as important that the students arrive at the correct classification of all rocks into three scientific groups. What is most important is that they develop several classification systems, have sound reasoning behind each system, and utilize more and more detailed observations with the

Figure 7.15   Student Sample Report

Rocks and Rock Classification

In the beginning we went by what we remembered from science this year. Some of the rocks we put into the right groups, but a lot of them were wrong. We had the basic idea of how to do the classification of the rocks. Some of the minerals looked more like sediment. It was sort of tough. The shiny, black one was hard to classify because it was black and had minerals in it.

During the rock experiment we made groups of igneous, sedimentary, and metamorphic rocks. We wrote some characteristics of each rock. We also wrote some characteristics of each group in general. Our group created an easy-to-use dichotomous key that would work for almost any rock. It started at layers and no layers, which took out sedimentary. Then it went to crystals and shine, and not crystals and shine, which took our indigenous sedimentary.

Figure 7.16

development of each system. You could have the small groups turn in all of their classification systems along with written rationales even though they are only presenting one to the class.

• When students research the scientific rock groups, there are several opportunities for both formal and informal assessment.

- Research skills can either be taught in conjunction with this lesson and then informally assessed throughout the process or, if skills have been taught earlier, the research component can serve as a formal language grade.

- Formal presentation of the group's research findings can serve as an oral communication grade, if oral presentations are made, or as a written communication grade if a full school display case is created.

- Science content can also be formally assessed through either the oral presentation or the written display (or both if you have time). Again, you are looking for group label, group characteristics, and formation specifically. The cycle of change and how it relates to rock types may also be assessed either informally or incorporated formally into the requirements of the research depending on the grade level.

EXTENSIONS AND MODIFICATIONS

If this lesson goes well, consider starting a school science museum with several other student-generated displays. Museums can be set up in an extra classroom (should such an anomaly exist in your school!) or in an atrium or wide hallway. Student groups could also develop interactive exhibits so that other students in the school could learn from hands-on participation in the museum. For example, following this research on rock types, groups could develop a "Guide to Rock Identification" with pictures of typical rocks in each group and key characteristics to help other students know if a rock belongs in that group. They could put out some new rocks (those not identified in the display collections) for students to figure out, or other students could be encouraged to bring in rocks that they would like to identify and use the resources to do that.

SUGGESTED READINGS AND RESOURCES

Parker, S., Visscher, P., Hewetson, N. J., & Turvey, R. (1997). *Eyewitness explorers: Rocks and minerals.* New York: DK Publishing.

Ricciuti, E. & Carruthers, M. (1998). *Rocks and minerals.* Englewood Cliffs, NJ: Scholastic.

Stewart, M. (2002). *Igneous rocks.* Portsmouth, NH: Heinneman.

Stewart, M. (2002). *Metamorphic rocks.* Portsmouth, NH: Heinneman.

Stewart, M. (2002). *Sedimentary rocks.* Portsmouth, NH: Heinneman.

Symes, R. F. (2000). *Eyewitness rocks and minerals.* New York: DK Publishing.

VOCABULARY

igneous rock: rocks formed primarily through cooling magma; characterized by crystals and/or air pockets

metamorphic rock: rocks formed through constant heat and pressure over time

sedimentary rock: rocks formed through layering of sediments, which become pressed/cemented together over time

ACADEMIC STANDARDS

Grade Level: 3–6

Science:

Observing for details (NS.K–4.1 and NS.5–8.1 Science as Inquiry)

Classifying rocks according to physical characteristics (NS.K–4.4 and NS.5–8.4 Earth and Space Science)

Identifying rock groups by characteristics and formation patterns (NS.K–4.4 and NS.5–8.4 Earth and Space Science)

Discuss how rocks fit into a cycle of change (NS.K–4.4 and NS.5–8.4 Earth and Space Science)

Language:

Sharing information from research orally (ENG.K–12.4 Communication Skills)

Publishing written information based on research (ENG.K–12.5 Communication Strategies)

Researching information about rock types (ENG.K–12.7 Evaluating Data and ENG.K–12.8 Developing Research Skills)

Social Studies:

Understand the physical processes that shape the patterns of Earth's surface (NCSS–G.K–12.3 Geography–Physical Systems)

Social Studies Lesson Plans

8

- ➤ I'M A MYSTERY: WHAT'S MY HISTORY?
- ➤ CAN YOU DIG HISTORY?
- ➤ WHERE IN AMERICA ARE YOU?
- ➤ FLOWER POWER

I'M A MYSTERY: WHAT'S MY HISTORY?

ESSENTIAL UNDERSTANDING

Big Idea: Perspective

Essential Understanding(s): Perspective is influenced by experience. The value a person gives to an object is determined by his or her perspective.

OBJECTIVES

Students will

- Make detailed observations of objects.
- Use those observations to formulate questions and hypotheses about the objects.
- Use observations, questions, and hypotheses to describe the history of the objects from a first-person (object) perspective.

MATERIALS

For this lesson you will need

- Several antique tools that are unusual enough that students won't recognize them or be able to immediately determine their use
- Recording sheets for observations, questions, and hypotheses (found at the end of the lesson)
- Index cards or paper on which students will write out their history description

TIME REQUIRED

The time needed depends on the number of objects you use. I typically allow about five minutes per object (i.e., six objects would take thirty minutes.) with about fifteen minutes at the end for the groups to write their first-person narrative and about fifteen minutes to share the stories and reveal the true usage of the objects.

Figure 8.1   Sources for Objects: Antique Tools

Tools can be obtained relatively inexpensively from local antique stores or from older local residents. Both of these sources should be able to give you plenty of information about the object's use and history. An alternative to collecting the tools yourself would be to have students bring in objects of this nature. In rural areas, students may have access to old farm tools or be able to talk with grandparents about household tools they still have around. In more urban or suburban areas, the focus could be more on household implements or tools utilized in a particular trade or factory setting. In either case, be sure to talk with someone about the object to ensure accuracy in recounting its history and usage.

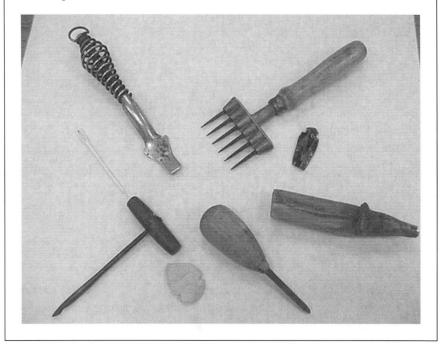

PROCEDURE

1. If the room is not already arranged into groups, move student desks together so that students can easily work together in small groups. The number of groups you have will obviously be dependent upon the number of objects you have for the students, but ideally there would be only three to four students in each group.

2. Give each group one of the antique tools from your collection. While it is easy to store and distribute these objects in clear plastic bags, you'll want to make sure that students are able to take the tools out of the plastic bags and touch them. This sensory experience will help many students in making their observations and formulating their questions and hypotheses.

Figure 8.2   Caution

It is very important to choose tools which will be safe in the classroom. Sharp points or parts which clamp and may pinch should be avoided with younger students or supervised very carefully with older students.

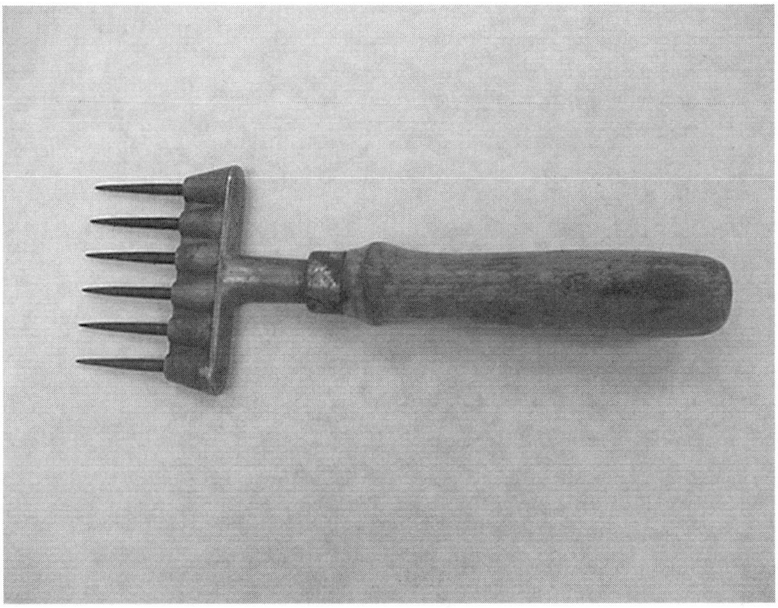

Provide a recording sheet on which students will record their observations, questions, and hypotheses. This can be set up in many ways, but I usually choose to have one recording sheet per object. This sheet then stays with the object instead of traveling with the group. In this way other groups can view previous groups' ideas.

3. Tell students that their job is to tell the story of the object. In order to do this, ask the student groups to examine the tool very carefully. There should be one recorder in the group who writes down everyone's observations (while still contributing his or her own, of course!). Observations and questions should all be recorded on the recording sheet (see Figure 8.3). Since I usually do this lesson at the very beginning of the school year, I usually provide students with a few guiding questions to get them thinking but ask them to also come up with their own. As the year progresses, I often repeat this lesson with different tools. For this first lesson, I do provide some guiding questions but with later applications of the lesson I have the students take on more of the responsibility for developing the questions about the object. After recording brainstorming information, the group should record their hypothesis and answers to the questions on the recording sheet (Figure 8.3).

Figure 8.3   Recording Sheet: I'm a Mystery: What's My History?

Object 1:

Group 1:

What is it called?
Who used it?
How was it used?
How do you know?
Why was it discarded?

Group 2:

What is it called?
Who used it?
How was it used?
How do you know?
Why was it discarded?

Group 3:

What is it called?
Who used it?
How was it used?
How do you know?
Why was it discarded?

Group 4:

What is it called?
Who used it?
How was it used?
How do you know?
Why was it discarded?

Group 5:

What is it called?
Who used it?
How was it used?
How do you know?
Why was it discarded?

Group 6 Notes:

---

4.   After the groups have had enough time to thoroughly investigate the first tool, I ask them to rotate to another object, leaving the recording sheet behind with the object.

5.   Student groups repeat the process with all of the tools provided. The way I set up this lesson, each group who visits an object can see what all previous groups have thought and recorded about the object. The stipulation I make is that each group must read what all previous groups recorded, but they may not come up with the same hypothesis about what the object is. They may, of course, have similar observations and questions, but their final hypothesis about what the object is and was used for must be unique.

6.   When groups arrive at their last object, the directions change. I ask students to do a little more with this tool. Students must read through everything that the others have contributed and may or may not use that to write a descriptive history of the object. I tell them that they may combine ideas from other groups or may add ideas of their own. This last group writes up the object's personal history or story using first-person perspective ("I am a _____, and I was used by _____.").

7.   After groups have had time to develop and write their stories, I ask students to share their work. I ask them to begin by sharing their observations and questions and then to read their story.

8.   Following the group share time, I do tell them what the objects actually are and how they were used. This may take a little reading/research on your part, but usually the antique dealer from whom you purchased the tools will be able to tell you a great deal about their functions.

9.   I then engage the students in a discussion about the value of objects and the role of perspective in determining the value of objects to each individual.

Questions typically used in these discussions are found in the Discussion Questions section below.

ADAPTATIONS

• Have students keep their recording sheet with them as they travel from object to object so that their observations, questions, and hypotheses are not shared with others. When all objects have been analyzed, have groups share their thoughts about each tool prior to you revealing its

Figure 8.4   Student Sample

Group 1:

What is it called?	Clothes pin
Who used it?	China people
How was it used?	To hang clothes
How do you know?	Looks like a clothes pin
Why was it discarded?	It was too big

Group 2:

What is it called?	pliers
Who used it?	colonists
How was it used?	If something was stuck it would pull it out.
How do you know?	Because it opens and closes like one
Why was it discarded?	Because it didn't work

Group 3:

What is it called?	Skin clip
Who used it?	dinosaurs
How was it used?	To clip skin
How do you know?	Because it looks like one
Why was it discarded?	It was too small

Group 4:

What is it called?	Hair clip
Who used it?	Madonna
How was it used?	To put up your hair
How do you know?	It has two clips and a spring
Why was it discarded?	It went out of style

Group 5:

What is it called?	The snapper
Who used it?	parents
How was it used?	To discipline bad kids
How do you know?	Because it hurts
Why was it discarded?	It broke

Group 6:

I am a clothes pin. I was used by everyone for the purpose of hanging clothes. You can tell this by the way I'm shaped. I was discarded because a better one was made.

actual name and function. Lead a discussion about the similarities and differences in the groups' recordings and link this to perspective.

• Have students bring in tools from their homes or neighborhoods for use in the same lesson. Students will be invested in facilitating the other students' discoveries about their object.

Figure 8.5   Language Tie-In

Presenting history through a story-telling approach is very appealing to students, especially those who "claim" not to like history! All students love to listen to stories, and you can capture the interest of those who have a love of language and writing through this activity.

Figure 8.6   Sample Student Report

Observation Story

The times were hard that year on the Nebraska prairie. Billy had been out of work for 16 months. But he never missed dinner. His favorite food—fried, crinkly potato chips. And that's where I come in. I'm a potato slicer. I have a beautiful scarlet handle, ergonomically designed for the tired housewife. My wood's texture is smooth, gentle, yet strong. My corrugated blade allows for beautifully sliced potatoes that are transformed into the world's greatest potato chips.

• Use groupings of tools and have students investigate their similarities and differences. For example, you might collect tools related to particular trades found in a colonial town or particular jobs in an Indian village. All of the tools grouped together would have been used in the same trade/job, and the students' job would be to determine what that trade/job was and how the objects were utilized.

DISCUSSION QUESTIONS

1. How did your personal experiences influence your observations, questions, and hypotheses? (i.e., did you attribute modern uses to things from the past)

2. In what way(s) does knowing the "story" behind an object affect the value you give to the object?

I usually do the following quick activity to get this going:

I show students some small, white buttons—usually round, shell-type buttons—and tell them that I just picked them up at the dollar store. When I ask who wants them, typically no one (or very few) will have any interest in them. Then I change the story and tell them that the buttons came from their great, great-grandmother's wedding dress and that they are all that is left of the dress. Now when asked who wants them, most, if not all, hands go up.

What's the difference? How does history affect their perspective about the buttons?

ASSESSMENT AND EVALUATION

• I have groups identify themselves by number on the recording sheet so that I can review their observations, questions, and hypotheses. As this is an informal, group task typically done the first week of school, I do not assign grades to this stage although you could. I move from group to group assessing the comfort level of the students with regard to group work, working with objects, making observations, and formulating questions and hypotheses. In this way, I can ensure that all students are actively engaged in some way with the objects.

• I do give a grade on the descriptive history write-up about the object. You could ask for one write-up per group and give a group grade or ask students to write their own stories and give individual grades.

EXTENSIONS AND MODIFICATIONS

• Have students bring in their own objects/artifacts for analysis. They could bring in something that says something about them, and you might use it as a way for students to introduce themselves to the class during the first week. Other students could make observations about their object and formulate a question about it for the owner. Students could then ask questions of each other about their objects and determine why the object has value for the student who brought it in.

- Invite a local archaeologist into your classroom and ask him/her to bring in some unusual artifacts for the students to analyze. Again they could make observations, formulate questions, and develop hypotheses about the objects and their use(s).

- If using the groupings of objects, have students further investigate the trade or job through research. They could find out exactly how the objects were utilized, typical requirements for someone entering into the trade, and what types of products or services were created. You could even extend this into an economics lesson talking about different types of resources and supply and demand issues.

SUGGESTED READINGS AND RESOURCES

Griffith, D. (1994). *The many faces of truth.* East Windsor Hill, CT: Synergetics.
Barrett, K. (1996). *Investigating artifacts: Making masks, creating myths, exploring middens.* Don Mills, ON, Canada: Addison Wesley Longman.

VOCABULARY

artifact: any object which represents something from the past and gives some information about a culture

hypothesis: an educated explanation of what you think something is or why you think something happened; hypotheses should be based on your past observations and experiences

observations: observations do not involve any reasoning; they are simply recordings of information you take in through your senses

perspective: your point-of-view, or the way in which you view things, based on your own experiences and beliefs

ACADEMIC STANDARDS

Grade Level: 4–8

Social Studies:

"Read" artifacts.

Recognize and understand that history is a matter of perspective (NCSS-G.K–12.2 Geography–Places and Regions)

Science:

Observe for details (NS.K–4.1 and NS.5–8.1 Science as Inquiry)

Formulate questions based on observations (NS.K–4.1 and NS.5–8.1 Science as Inquiry)

Formulate hypotheses (NS.K–4.1 and NS.5–8.1 Science as Inquiry)

Language:

Use descriptive details in writing (ENG.K–12.5 Communication Strategies)

Distinguish and use first-person perspective (ENG.K–12.5 Communication Strategies)

Orally share information–within small group (ENG.K–12.4 Communication Skills)

Orally share information—report to large group (ENG.K–12.4 Communication Skills)

CAN YOU DIG HISTORY?

ESSENTIAL UNDERSTANDING

Big Idea: Perspective

Essential Understanding(s): Examining aspects of the daily life of a culture can provide insight into its people's perspective.

OBJECTIVES

Students will

- Uncover artifacts.
- "Read artifacts" to discover clues about the culture from which they came.
- Hypothesize about the characteristics of the culture to whom such artifacts would have belonged and the environment within which they lived.

MATERIALS

For this lesson you will need

- Large plastic tubs
- Heavy sand or soil (two different colors will be needed for the extension activity)
- Excavation tools including trowels, medium-sized paint brushes, and dustpans
- Objects representing a particular culture from a particular time period (this lesson focuses on two distinct cultures in colonial America, but you could use any cultures and any time period)
- Recording sheet for observations and hypotheses (found at the end of the lesson)

TIME REQUIRED

The time frame for this lesson depends on the level of your students and the number and complexity of objects they will be excavating. Typically the lesson can be done in two phases: (1) the excavation and recording session, which usually takes forty-five minutes to an hour, and (2) the

Figure 8.7   Sources for Objects: Colonial Artifacts

Many historic attractions sell replicas of artifacts that have been excavated during archaeological work on their sites. The "artifacts" here were purchased relatively inexpensively in Jamestown and Colonial Williamsburg. Many times there will be several versions of the same type of reproduction, for example, clay pipes; be sure to choose the least expensive one! There's no point in paying a lot for objects that you will most likely be breaking apart or "weathering" to make them look older! Also remember to look for souvenir-type items that could be taken apart and used for their component pieces. For example, I bought a cheap anklet made of shells and plastic pieces, took it apart, and kept just the shells, which were similar to those that would have been used by the local natives.

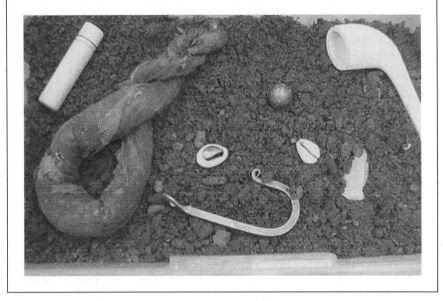

synthesis session, in which students first work in a small groups and then come together as a class to formulate hypotheses about how all of the different excavation units fit together. This generally lasts longer, perhaps two to three class periods of between forty-five minutes and one hour.

PROCEDURE

1. Group students into excavation teams and assign each team to a different excavation unit. This unit will be a plastic tub which you have put together with buried artifacts. Demonstrate proper excavation techniques—removing small layers of soil with a trowel and dust pan or brushing around artifacts with the paintbrush—so students will know how to work on their unit.

2. Tell students that although each team has its own unit to excavate, the units all come from the same overall site. That means that all of the artifacts will, in some way, connect with one another. The students' job at this point is to uncover the artifacts in their unit and hypothesize regarding three questions:

- What is the artifact?
- Who would have used it and how?
- What does the object indicate about the culture of the people who would have occupied the site at that time period?

They should record their observations and hypotheses on the group's recording sheet (Figure 8.8).

3. As students begin to excavate, you can move from group to group and facilitate by asking questions. You should not direct students toward a particular way of thinking or hypothesizing but should, instead, ask students for their thinking and pose questions which will return their focus to the objects themselves and what they have to "say."

4. It is important that student groups form their hypotheses prior to returning to share their ideas with the whole class. The way in which I construct my artifact boxes makes this particularly important. I have two very different cultures represented in the boxes—early Jamestown settlers from England and Powhatan Indians. Both of these perspectives will be very important in the class discussion. Frequently students will believe that they have it all easily figured out based on the artifacts in their box. They will either say it's a colonial settlement or it's a Native American village depending on what type of box they have excavated. When the groups come together, they realize that they must be very specific in identifying their site and that it must accommodate *all* of the artifacts. They are initially thrown by the mixture of artifacts from both cultures until finally they begin to think about all of the possibilities in which these two cultures come have come together.

5. After groups have had adequate time to excavate their artifacts and record their hypotheses, all groups should come back together to share their thoughts. Have each group show their artifacts and share their thinking about them as well as their hypothesis about what type of site these units represent. You should ask students what questions they have about the artifacts and encourage students to hypothesize answers to each other's questions. You can ask probing questions if the students

Figure 8.8   Recording Sheet: Can You Dig History?

Recording Sheet

After you have excavated your artifacts from your unit, make careful observations of each object. Record your observations in column one below. In column two, hypothesize what the artifact actually is or was. In column three, predict who would have used it and how. Finally, at the bottom, hypothesize what the objects together tell you about the culture group who occupied this site.

Observations	The artifact(s)/was . . .	Who would have used it? How?

Taken together, what could these objects tell you about the culture group who occupied this site?

Figure 8.9   Artifact Recommendations

I usually put seven or eight artifacts in each excavation unit/box. Fewer than this does not really provide adequate material from which to make hypotheses. You can make each box either entirely representative of one culture or, even more realistically, you could mix artifacts from different cultures in the boxes.

Good colonist artifacts include English money, belt/shoe buckles, bullets, clay pipes (break into pieces), buttons, and shoe leather/soles.

Good Powhatan artifacts include arrowheads, cowrie shells, corn kernels, leather products like thumb guards, gourd pieces, oyster shells, and pieces of clay pots.

remain confused for some time about the mix of artifacts from two cultures, but you should not reveal to students the interrelationships of the artifacts. The students should be able to uncover this for themselves through hearing each others' questions and hypotheses and seeing each group's artifacts.

ADAPTATIONS

This lesson involves early English colonists and Powhatan cultures. However, any two cultures that would have interacted—positively or negatively—can be used. I have also done this lesson with artifacts representing plantation owners and slaves. It could also be done with Native American cultures and Spanish conquistadors in the West. The possibilities are endless.

You could also do this lesson with focus on just one culture. To do this you would need to ensure that the artifacts chosen are not too obvious in order to provide the same opportunity for hypothesizing and critical thinking.

DISCUSSION QUESTIONS

For the majority of this lesson, the students will be developing the questions, and the teacher should follow the direction of the students. However, there are certain situations in which guiding or facilitating questions will be needed. For example, students typically know that arrowheads were used by Native Americans for hunting and protection but will not always make the connection to why they might be excavated along with early English artifacts. In order to get them to move closer to the idea that arrowheads may be found in an English settlement due to conflicts between the two groups, you might ask students questions like

1. What are all of the possibilities for how this object could have been used?

2. What groups of people typically used such an object?

3. With what other groups did these people come into contact? What was the nature of these interactions?

ASSESSMENT AND EVALUATION

Informally, many social studies skills can be assessed including observation and "reading" of artifacts, identifying elements of culture, and discussing cultural interactions.

Language skills such as summarizing and orally presenting information can also be informally assessed.

Formally, following the whole-class discussion, students can write a response to the activity specifically focusing on what the artifacts reveal about the two cultures and how the two cultures' perspectives would differ from one another. This would serve as both a social studies and a language evaluation. This written response could also include directions for the student to assume the perspective of a member of one culture or the other and tell the story of the site.

EXTENSIONS AND MODIFICATIONS

If time permits, you can use two different layers of soil (called strata) differentiated by their color. The top layer will represent one time period while the lower layer will represent an earlier period in time. Follow the same procedure as above but add the element that students are really looking at two different sites (or more accurately, the same site at two different time periods). Have them hypothesize what the site was used for first (lower layer) and then to what new use it was put later in time (top layer). This is, of course, easier to do with just one culture!

If you've collected enough artifacts to represent three or four different sites, you can provide student groups with artifacts and site information in a box and have them plan the excavation. They should prepare the excavation boxes by choosing and burying the artifacts (have them create a map first!) and should be prepared to lead the discussion (using their site information sheet) following the excavation. Each group would be preparing boxes for another group in the class so that during excavation everyone is engaged in the process. Following excavation, each group would take a turn sharing their findings, and the group who planned the site will lead the discussion. Take time to have discussion leaders prepare to lead their classmates through the explanation and discussion phases by helping them develop questions and showing them how to probe other students' thinking about the artifacts and their conclusions.

SUGGESTED READINGS AND RESOURCES

Archaeology: Digging Up History (1983). [special issue]. *Cobblestone Magazine,* 4(6).

Samford, P. & Ribblett, D. (1995). *Archaeology for young explorers.* Williamsburg, VA: Colonial Williamsburg Foundation.

For this lesson: Rediscovery Series published by Jamestown Publishers.

VOCABULARY

artifacts: objects that reveal something about the culture from which they came

excavation: the process of uncovering artifacts carefully from a site

hypothesis: a "guess" based on observations or factual information obtained from the artifact

ACADEMIC STANDARDS

Grade Level: 4–8

Social Studies:

"Read" artifacts

Observe historical objects

Investigate cultural perspective (NCSS-G.K–12.2 Geography–Places and Regions)

Investigate cultural interactions (NCSS-G.K–12.4 Geography–Human Systems)

Science:

Make observations (NS.K-4.1 & NS.5–8.1 Science as Inquiry)

Develop hypotheses and support with evidence (NS.K–4.1 and NS.5–8.1 Science as Inquiry)

Excavation processes (NS.K–4.1 and NS.5–8.1 Science as Inquiry)

Language:

Orally present and defend hypotheses–small group (ENG.K–12.4 Communication Skills)

Orally present and defend hypotheses–whole class (ENG.K–12.4 Communication Skills)

Write from a particular perspective (ENG.K–12.5 Communication Strategies)

WHERE IN AMERICA ARE YOU?

ESSENTIAL UNDERSTANDING:

Big Idea: Adaptation

Essential Understanding(s): Humans adapt to their environment. Available resources aid humans in adaptation. Available resources contribute to lifestyle.

OBJECTIVES

Students will

- Make detailed observations of photographs.
- Identify resources used in lifestyle objects found in photographs (housing, clothes, art objects, etc.).
- Predict geographic location depicted in photographs.
- Justify predictions with concrete examples of resource identification and knowledge of geographic features.
- Share predictions and justification with a small group and with the class.

MATERIALS

For this lesson you will need

- Photographs of Native American lifestyle objects representing all regions of the United States (NW, SW, Plains, NE, SE, and Arctic)
- Recording sheet for writing resources observed and predictions (found at the end of the lesson plan)
- Large map of the United States

TIME REQUIRED

The time frame for this lesson depends on when in a Native American or geography unit you use it. If used as an initial assessment to determine what students know about the climate and other geographical features of particular regions, it might be completed in one social studies lesson of perhaps forty-five minutes. If used as a culminating exercise in which students should have more information about geographic features, it could take two to three class periods (forty-five minutes each). I suggest

Figure 8.10 Sources for Objects: Photographs

The best place I have found for Native American photographs from all regions is the Smithsonian Institution's Museum of the American Indian in New York. The gift shop in this museum sells postcard collections that contain photographs from a wide variety of Native American tribes, but you will need to know which tribes come from which region. (The museum also has a vast quantity of excellent resources from each region that can help you identify tribes with which you are not familiar).

Another possible way to get such photographs is to contact people you know who might be traveling to a particular region. They might be able to bring photograph postcards back from their travels. Of course, this only provides a limited number of photographs from one region, and you will need to provide a very specific description of what you plan to use the photos for so that you get pictures that contain useable "information."

Figure 8.11 Set-Up Tip

If postcard sets are used, the name of the tribe and possibly even the geographic location of the tribe will be found on the back of each card. While most students won't recognize many of the tribal names, some students may be familiar with some of them and others will be recognizable to the majority of the class (e.g., Sioux). If students read the back of the postcards prior to completing the lesson, they will have less opportunity to make predictions. Therefore I suggest that you glue the postcards to sheets of construction paper, and number them on the back. Be sure to identify the tribe name and any other pertinent information next to the photograph number on a separate answer key!

that it be used as a combination culminating geography lesson and introductory Native American lesson, and I usually spend three forty-five-minute class periods on the lesson.

PROCEDURE

1. Gather a collection of photographs together and sort them into piles according to the region from which the tribe depicted comes. There should be a wide variety of different pictures in each pile, some showing housing, some depicting clothing, others representing artistic objects. Place each group of photographs into a separate plastic bag labeled just with a group number.

2. Provide student groups with one bag containing photographs representing one geographic region. Ask them to take out the pictures and

examine them carefully looking for clues about what region is represented in the photographs. Provide each group with a recording sheet on which to write down the things they see, what those items might tell them about the region in which the tribes live(d), and how the tribe used the depicted resources to adapt to their environment (see Figure 8.12).

3. Provide students with sufficient time to examine photographs (you might want to provide magnifying glasses for closer examination). Circulate among the groups making sure that students are recording information on the recording sheets appropriately. They should be identifying not only what objects they see in the photographs but also what resources seem to have been used (adaptation) and what that object tells them about the region from which the tribe came/comes.

4. Once students have finished recording their information, have them prepare a short presentation for the class about their prediction and rationale. Each student could present a particular photograph depicting key information which led them to determine that the photographs in their bag represented a particular region. What you expect out of this presentation will obviously depend on at what point in the lesson it is done. If you are using this as a pre-assessment to determine what students already know about climate and geographical features found in particular regions, you would not expect the same level of detail as you would if you choose to use this as a culminating exercise at the end of a geography unit.

ADAPTATIONS

Have students work through this activity at the beginning of an integrated unit on regional geography and Native American culture. When students present their hypotheses and rationales, do not tell them whether they are correct or not in their predictions. Once the unit is complete and students have more information both in terms of geography and lifestyles of different groups of Native Americans, have them revisit their photograph set and prediction sheet. See if they want to revise their prediction based on their new knowledge. Have them present their findings and prediction again and discuss if/how it changed.

DISCUSSION QUESTIONS

Depending on the overall ability and experience levels of the students you're teaching, they will need some help moving from identifying resources seen in the photograph to hypothesizing what that resource

Figure 8.12   Recording Sheet: Where in America Are You?

Recording Sheet

In the first column record what you see in the photographs (e.g., a shield). In the second column record the resources you believe were used to make the item (e.g., some kind of thick animal hide). Finally, in the third column hypothesize what the environment would be like that would support that resource (e.g., the climate must be colder, at least at times, and the terrain must be rugged because the animal hide must be very thick if it's used for protection)

Observations	Resources Used	Hypotheses About Environment

Figure 8.13   Resource Suggestion

It is often helpful to have a large map of the United States available so that students can use this to make their predictions. They can see where bodies of water or mountain ranges are as well as obtain general latitude and longitude information for each region.

could tell them about the region. In examining a picture of a clay pot, for example, some students will tell you simply that it means that there is clay in the region instead of mentioning the indication of the proximity to water or thinking about what that type of soil would mean for growing things.

Your questions will need to guide students in moving from their observations toward in-depth hypotheses about regional characteristics. For example,

1. What does the fact that they're wearing fur coats tell you? (Probe for information about colder climate, presence of particular animals, use of all parts of an animal.)

2. What would the presence of the clay (used to make this pot) prevent in this region? (Probe for connections to ability to engage in farming.)

3. What else would be needed in the region to turn the clay into this pot? (Probe for proximity to water, temperature issues.)

ASSESSMENT AND EVALUATION

Whether or not you formally evaluate this activity will be determined to a great extent by at what point in the unit it is used:

• Obviously, if it is used solely as a pre-assessment, that is its purpose, and the results should not be evaluated.

• However, if it is used as a culminating activity or if the alternative suggestion above is used, various parts of the lesson can be evaluated. I would not evaluate the students based on whether or not they identify the correct region. I would instead evaluate their thinking processes and the rationale they provide for their prediction. This can be done individually as well by having each student present their argument in writing prior to the group's presentation.

Figure 8.14   Sample of Student Work

I think that these objects came from an Indian tribe. It is probably very cold where they lived because the clothing is thick. The hood comes tight over the face to stay warm. They also probably lived in the woodlands because many of the items are made of wood. Lots of items are made with dye, which may have come from berries. There are streams and some lakes near the woods. The basket is made from reeds that would grow near water. There is a feather hat. It's probably from birds migrating north. This tribe probably lived in the northwest.

—Karin, Grade 5

• If the alternative strategy above is used, you can also assess growth from beginning to end of the unit.

• Oral presentation skills can be formally evaluated as part of the language arts curriculum.

• The more distinctive photographs could also be used as a formal evaluation tool by putting them up on the overhead or taped to the board and having students identify the region each represents and provide a rationale for choosing a particular region for each picture.

EXTENSIONS AND MODIFICATIONS

• Once the prediction and presentation has been completed, do not provide students with the correct answer. Instead have them engage in a collaborative research quest to find out whether they are correct. Using their observations from the "objects" themselves (photographs) to guide them, they can research each region until they feel certain that they have either verified or rejected their original hypothesis. (You could use either geography resources, Native American resources, or both here). If they reject their hypothesis, they should be able justify why as well as provide information as to what region they now believe is correct. If they verify their prediction, they should be able to back this up with research documentation.

• Give each individual student one or two photographs and have them individually complete steps three and four above. After everyone has presented, have students break into groups according to the regions they predicted for their photographs. Students can then look at the collection of photographs and discuss whether they all belong in the same group or not by looking for general themes or patterns in the photos. Those who decide that their photo doesn't actually belong in the group, can transfer to a new group. Continue this process until all students feel that their photos fit well within the group of photos they believe represents a region.

SUGGESTED READINGS AND RESOURCES

Griffin-Pierce, T. (1995). *The encyclopedia of Native America.* New York: Viking.

Perdue, T. & Green, M. (2001). *The Columbia guide to American Indians of the Southwest.* New York: Columbia University Press.

Press, P. (1997). *Indians of the Northwest: Traditions, history, legends, and life.* Philadelphia: Courage.

Sita, L. (1997). *Indians of the Great Plains: Traditions, history, legends, and life.* Philadelphia: Courage.

Sita, L. (1997). *Indians of the Northeast: Traditions, history, legends, and life.* Philadelphia: Courage.

Sita, L. (1997). *Indians of the Southwest: Traditions, history, legends, and life.* Philadelphia: Courage.

Time-Life. (1994). *People of the ice and snow.* New York: Time-Life.

Viola, H. (1996). *North American Indians.* New York: Crown.

VOCABULARY

adaptation: change made over time to accommodate or adjust to one's environment

observations: observations do not involve any reasoning; they are simply recordings of information you take in through your senses

rationale/justification: the reasoning that exists to back up something that is claimed or offered as a hypothesis

region: a geographic area differentiated from other geographic areas by particular land or water features, climate, and resources

resources: natural or man-made objects used in the production of some other object or tool

ACADEMIC STANDARDS

Grade Level: 3–6

Social Studies:

"Read" photographs

Recognize adaptation to a geographical region (NCSS–G.K–12.5 Geography–Environment and Society)

Explain the impact of physical geography on humans' resource utilization (NCSS-G.K–12.5 Geography–Environment and Society)

Science:

Observe for details (NS.K–4.1 and NS.5–8.1 Science as Inquiry)

Formulate hypotheses based on evidence(NS.K–4.1 and NS.5–8.1 Science as Inquiry)

Identify natural resources (NS.K–4.3 and NS.5–8.3 Life Science)

Language:

Orally share information—within small group (ENG.K–12.4 Communication Skills)

Orally share information—report to a large group (ENG.K–12.4 Communication Skills)

FLOWER POWER

ESSENTIAL UNDERSTANDING

Big Idea: People create regions to interpret Earth's complexity

Essential Understanding: The regions of the United States were created based on the geographic differences within the United States including climate, soils, vegetation and landforms.

OBJECTIVES

Students will

- Determine the area of the United States that a plant came from using information found in a field guide of flowers.
- Collect, record, and report data using maps of the United States.
- Understand that plants thrive in different environments.

MATERIALS

For this lesson you will need

- Pictures and descriptions of flowers from different biomes in the United States (using state flowers makes this an easier task)
- A map of the United States
- Characteristics of biomes table
- Crayons, markers, or colored pencils
- Drawing paper
- Resource materials, including Internet access if possible, to help students discover the biome in which their flowers
- Field guides for flowers, including on-line field guides
- Large map of the United States
- Small sticky notes

PROCEDURE

A discussion or lesson on the different biomes found in the United States is necessary before you begin this lesson.

Figure 8.15   Sources for Objects: Flower Power

This collection took me a little while to put together. First, I tried to find flowers that could be found only in one biome. Then I tried to find pictures that could be copied easily on the copier. I included a description of the flower with information that would help the students make a reasonable prediction about where the flower could be found in the country. This was difficult until I came across a book with state flowers, which helped me find flowers by region. Choose carefully though, because not all state flowers are unique to the region the state is found in.

1. Place students in groups of four or five.

2. Place resource books in a central area.

3. Distribute pictures and descriptions of flowers from different regions of the United States (see Figure 8.16), data worksheets (see Figure 8.17), and biomes data (see Figure 8.18) to each group. Use pictures and descriptions of one to five flowers from each region per group. Use flowers that have biological needs typical to the regions, such as those from the Southwest region which are tolerant of dry, hot weather and minimum water and which thrive in sandy soil.

4. Working in groups, students will make observations about their flowers. They will record their observations on the worksheet. Flowers they think came from the same area will be grouped together. A prediction will be made as to which areas of the United States their flowers come from and three reasons will be given as to why they think so. A list will be generated and recorded of questions they think they need to have answered before they can make the final determination of the region from which the flowers came.

5. Students will present their findings to the class. The questions generated by each group, which students may draw upon for the next step, will be listed on the board.

6. Based on their predictions, students will begin research to verify their prediction. They will change their predictions as they find research to back them up.

7. Flowers will be drawn and colored on white drawing paper, or students will type out the information they have found at the bottom of a page and draw the picture of the flower at the top of the page.

Figure 8.16

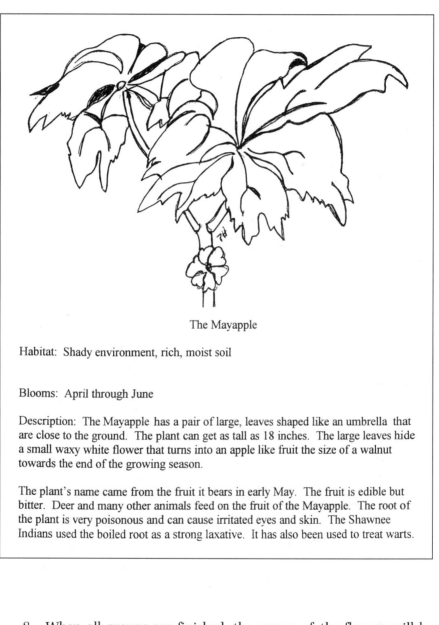

The Mayapple

Habitat: Shady environment, rich, moist soil

Blooms: April through June

Description: The Mayapple has a pair of large, leaves shaped like an umbrella that are close to the ground. The plant can get as tall as 18 inches. The large leaves hide a small waxy white flower that turns into an apple like fruit the size of a walnut towards the end of the growing season.

The plant's name came from the fruit it bears in early May. The fruit is edible but bitter. Deer and many other animals feed on the fruit of the Mayapple. The root of the plant is very poisonous and can cause irritated eyes and skin. The Shawnee Indians used the boiled root as a strong laxative. It has also been used to treat warts.

8. When all groups are finished, the names of the flowers will be written on small sticky notes and placed on a large map of the United States. Similarities will be noted, including growing conditions for the flowers.

9. Students will predict boundary lines for the regions of the United States based on their "flower map." The actual boundaries will be drawn on the map.

Figure 8.17 Student-Generated Data Worksheet: Flower Power

Questions About Our Flowers
1. What are they used for?
2. Are any of them used for food?
3. Are any of them used for medicine?
4. What conditions make the flowers grow in their habitat?
5. What gives the flowers their color or special protection?
6. How do the different plants attract pollinators?
7. How do the plants defend themselves from predators?
8. What types of adaptations do the flowers need to grow in the biomes they live in?
9. What temperatures do the plants live in?
10. How long are the plants roots?
11. What other plants live in the same area?
12. What kind of animals would eat them?
13. How much rain do they need to grow?
14. How long is the growing season?
15. Do they go dormant?
16. What kind of plants go dormant?

Figure 8.18

	Average Temperature	Precipitation	Vegetation	Other
Temperate Deciduous Forest	-30 C to 30 C, yearly average is 10 C, hot summers, cold winters	750 to 1500 mm of rain per year	broadleaf trees, shrubs, perennial flowers, mosses	have 4 seasons with leaves changing color, and falling off in winter, grow back in spring
Coniferous Forest	-40 C to 20 C, average summer temp is 10C	300 to 900 mm of rain per year	evergreen trees	cold, long, snowy winters and humid summers, well defined seasons
Grassland	-20 C to 30 C	500 to 900 mm of rain per year	grasses, clover, salvia, oats	
Desert	38 C (day) -3.9 C (night)	about 250 mm of rain per year	cacti, small bushes, short grasses	perennials survive by becoming dormant and then flourishing when water is available
Tundra	-40 C to 18 C	150 to 250 mm of rain per year		coldest biomes, tundra is from the Finnish meaning "treeless plain"

Figure 8.19

Name of Plant	Description	Habitat	Add't. Info.	Uses	Plant Height
Ironweed	dark purple thistle-like w/o thorns	grasslands	moist meadows		8 ft.
Beggarweed	violet, magenta and sometimes white	deciduous forest	quail and turkeys feed on	help restore fertility	1-4 ft.
Wintergreen	small, shiny, deep green leaves	coniferous forest	has evergreen trees	fragrant	2-5 ft.
Gromwell	white, yellow	grasslands	common in open fields	purple dye	1-3 ft.
Prickly poppy	large white or yellow blooms, sharp prickles	dry places	can survive hot, dry climates	bitter juice	2-3 ft.
Arrowhead	while, lily-like flowers, arrow-shaped leaves	marsh and aquatic plants	along ponds and slow streams	food for ducks, Indians, and early settlers	1-2 ft.

DISCUSSION QUESTIONS

1. What do all plants need to survive?

2. Do all plants have the same needs?

3. What insects or animals depend on the plant or does the plant depend on for pollination? Does knowing this help determine the region?

4. What kind of map could be used to find out what the average temperatures or rainfall are in the different regions of the United States?

EVALUATION

Students will be evaluated informally as a group on

- Working cooperatively
- Staying on task
- Completion of plant data sheet

The individual students will be formally evaluated for

- Knowledge of why regions are established (through writing a journal entry)
- Knowledge of geographic characteristics of the regions of the United States
- Students will be given a variety of flowers to place into the appropriate regions of the United States based on the biome in which the plant lives.
- Short written report about the flower they researched, including a description of the flower, the biome it lives in, the region of the United States it can be found in, and answers to any questions they researched

EXTENSIONS

- This activity can be done in conjunction with the study of biomes in science.

- For a study of world geography, information about plants from around the world could be collected.

- Instead of just flowers, other plants could be included, such as trees, grasses, and more.

- This activity could be included in a unit on plants.

SUGGESTED READINGS AND RESOURCES

Cooper, J. (1997). *The Rourke guide to state symbols.* Vero Beach, FL: Rourke.
eNature. Online field guides. Retrieved May 2002, from www.enature.com
Martin, L. (1998). *Wild flower folklore.* Chester, CT: Globe Pequot.
NASA. Earth observatory laboratory: Mission: Biomes. Retrieved May 2002, from
      http://www.earthobservatory.nasa.gov/Laboratory/Biome
Newcomb, L. (1977). *Newcomb's wildflower guide.* Boston: Little, Brown.
Zim, H. S. & Martin, A. C. (1991). *Flowers.* New York: Golden.

VOCABULARY

biome: a community of plants and animals living together in a certain environment

distinguishing characteristics: the characteristics of something that makes it unique and different from other things

opposite leaves: a pair of leaves growing from the same node, one on each side of the stem

node: the part of the stem where leaves begin to grow

coniferous forest: evergreen trees that produce cones and needles all year long

deciduous forest: broadleaf trees whose leaves change color with the season, fall off in autumn, and grow back in spring

ACADEMIC STANDARDS

Grade Level: 4–8

Social Studies (National Geography Standards):

How to use maps and other geographic representations, acquire tools and technologies, and process and report information (NS.K–12 Geography 1)

How to use mental maps to organize information about people, places, and environments (NS.K–12 Spatial Terms 2)

How to analyze the spatial organization of people, places, and environments on Earth's surface (NS.K–12 Spatial Terms 3)

The physical and human characteristics of places (Places and Regions 4)

That people create regions to interpret Earth's complexity (NS.K–12 Places and Regions 5)

The characteristics and spatial distribution of ecosystems on Earth's surface (NS.K–12 Physical Systems 8)

Math (National Standards)

Formulate questions that can be addressed with data, and display relevant data to answer questions (DA.5–8.1)

Develop and evaluate inferences and predictions that are based on data (DA.5–8.4)

Science (National Standards)

Structure and function in living systems (NS.5–8.3)

Diversity and adaptations of organisms (NS.5–8.3)

Math Lesson Plans 9

- ➢ MEASURING MADNESS
- ➢ ARCHITECTURAL GEOMETRY
- ➢ WHAT'S FOR DINNER?
- ➢ WHAT PART OF FRACTIONS IS DIFFICULT?

MEASURING MADNESS

ESSENTIAL UNDERSTANDING

Big Idea: Measurement systems

Essential Understanding: Measurement systems, including customary and metric, are based on standard units.

OBJECTIVES

Students will

- Discover that all measurement systems are based on a standard unit of measure.
- Recognize that the metric system is based on units of 1, 10, 100, and 1000 because it is so easy to convert measurements using 10 as a base.

MATERIALS

For this lesson you will need

- Linking one-inch cubes
- Large drawing paper
- Math resource books
- Crayons, markers, or colored pencils

TIME REQUIRED

The time required for this lesson will vary based on how long you give the students to work on the advertisement they will create. I give my students about forty-five minutes to complete the measuring task and design their advertisement for their measuring system. I give them one more forty-five-minute class period to complete the advertisement on the computer or by hand.

PROCEDURE

1. Give each student in the class one linking cube. Instruct the students to measure a variety of objects (a pencil, an eraser, their finger, a

Figure 9.1   Sources for Objects: Measurement

I have always found teaching measurement a real challenge, even when using a hands-on approach. No matter how many objects I give students to measure, when it comes to evaluation, they have trouble recalling the different units of measure, such as twelve inches in a foot and three feet to a yard. Teaching the metric system has been like teaching students a new language they don't want to learn. So, I designed this lesson, as frustrating as it may be at times for my students, to help them understand how easy the metric system is and to help them to remember the different units of measure and what they are used for.

For this lesson, I used multi-link cubes so the students can attach their units of measurement. These are available from any school supply company. A number of them are also included in many math kits provided with your math text book. However, if you don't have them, using any consistent unit will work, such as paper that you have pre-measured and cut out, or any other commercial linking block will work.

piece of chalk, etc.) using the cube. They should record their data. Students may choose objects to measure using the cube.

2. Next, give the students objects to measure that are a little larger (their desks, a book, the width of the chalkboard or a bulletin board, a floor tile, etc.). At this point, you may have students getting a little impatient with measuring objects with such a small unit of measure. Ask those students what they could do to the block to make the task easier. Students will probably suggest adding more blocks to the one unit.

3. Tell students they may add blocks, but they may add them only one time, and to choose the number of blocks to add wisely. They will need to give their new measuring tool a new name. They should then continue to measure the larger objects.

4. Next, give the students a larger task, such as measuring the distance from your classroom to a distant point, such as the library or cafeteria, using their measuring tool. Again, they should get frustrated, come up with a new unit of measure, and add that to their current measuring tool. They should give this tool a new name.

5. When students have successfully completed this task, they should be asked to reflect on how they solved their measurement tool problems. They should think about what the perfect measurement system would have and how big each unit should be. They should be reminded that school children everywhere will have to learn their measurement system,

Figure 9.2

Measure the following items using your unit cube:

1. a piece of chalk _____

2. a pencil _____

3. your math book _____

4. the width of your chair _____

Then measure:

5. the length of the blackboard _____

6. the width of the classroom _____

7. the length of the sink area _____

Then measure:

8. from our classroom to the office _____

9. the width of the hallway _____

10. the length of the carpet _____

so it shouldn't be too complicated. They should write their system down as a proposal to give you to for approval.

6. After giving students approval for appropriate measurement systems, they will design an ad to sell their system to the rest of the class. It should explain the system and tell the class why they should adopt their unit of measure. With luck, at least one student will come up with a system based on 10s. If not, you can lead them to this through questioning (see guiding questions).

7. Students will present their system to the class. Many of the systems may be similar. This can lead to further discussion about why a system of

Figure 9.3   Reflections

> In the beginning, it was easy to measure the short objects with one cube. Then we were stumped when we found out how long the second set of objects was to measure. We thought of using a math book, then multiplying. Then we decided to change the amount of cubes we used. I changed it to 20. The next set of items was even bigger. I used 40 cubes. It would have been easier with 50 or 100.

measurement based on 10s is a good choice. The class will vote on the measurement system they think would be the easiest to use and remember.

The students should now be prepared for a unit on customary and metric measurement, and should find this concept much easier to grasp.

DISCUSSION QUESTIONS

I usually just give my students the task and let them start measuring with nothing but the worksheet in front of them. I have the students work individually in small groups. They usually start getting frustrated about the same time, and this starts a discussion among them, which eventually includes asking me if they can add cubes to their unit of measurement. Before answering them, I usually ask them why they want to add cubes and what kind of problems they are having measuring with only one cube. Other discussion questions might include

- Why is one unit of measurement inappropriate for larger measurements?
- How could you come up with a system that is easy to remember?
- Which multiplication table is the easiest to remember? (10s)
- What makes your system easy to use and remember? Why will the class vote for it?

ASSESSMENT AND EVALUATION

Although an assessment can be taken on the advertisement the students create as part of a language assessment, the real evaluation will be the student's understanding and comprehension of the metric system, which will be introduced in the next math unit. However, students should understand from this activity:

- A consistent unit of measure needs to be utilized by everyone so measurements can be shared for a variety of purposes.
- Small units of measure are not accurate when measuring large objects or distances.

SUGGESTED READINGS

Ardley, N. (1983). *Making metric measurements.* New York: Watts.
Lasky, K. (1994). *The librarian who measured the Earth.* Boston: Little Brown.
Ling, B. (1997). *The fattest, tallest, biggest snowman ever.* New York: Scholastic.

ACADEMIC STANDARDS

Grade Level: 3–8

Math:

Understand such attributes as length and select the appropriate type of unit for measuring each attribute (NM-MEA.3–5.1)

Understand the need for measuring with standard units and become familiar with standard units in the customary and metric systems (NM-MEA.3–5.1)

Understand both metric and customary systems of measurement (NM-MEA.6–8.1)

Understand relationships among units and convert from one unit to another within the same system (NM-MEA.6–8.1)

Use common benchmarks to select appropriate methods for estimating measurements (NM-MEA.6–8.2)

ARCHITECTURAL GEOMETRY

ESSENTIAL UNDERSTANDING:

Big Idea: Balance

Essential Understandings: Balance can be aesthetically pleasing. Balance is necessary for structural integrity.

OBJECTIVES

Students will

- Identify geometric shapes.
- Distinguish between different types of triangles.
- Distinguish between plane and solid figures.
- Analyze buildings to determine the most frequently used geometric shapes in architecture.
- Evaluate buildings to determine the most aesthetically pleasing uses of geometric shapes in architecture.

MATERIALS

This is actually several lessons combined into a unit entitled Architectural Geometry. The resources have been identified by individual lessons within the unit.

Lesson One

- Several pre-cut triangles representing all three types (scalene, equilateral, isosceles)—one bag for each student or pair of students. (It is a good idea to xerox the triangles on heavy tag board or laminate them if you make them out of construction paper. This will ensure durability when being handled by students.)
- Rulers and protractors for each student or pair of students
- Pictures of buildings which clearly show the use of triangles (pediments, dormer windows, some rooflines, etc.). (You might want to tie these pictures in with a social studies unit such as Colonial America.)

Lesson Two

- Plane figures cut out of construction paper
- Sets of solid figures containing most basic shapes (cube, rectangular prism, triangular prism, sphere, cone, cylinder)
- Photographs or slides of buildings with distinct architectural features in which geometric shapes can be clearly identified

Hands-On Task

- Disposable cameras, one per group of three to four students
- Access to buildings for photographing

OR

- Chart paper, one large piece per group of three to four students
- Construction paper
- Scissors, glue, rulers, protractors for each group
- Chart models of construction designs for building

TIME REQUIRED

The first lesson requires very little time. Assuming that students are facile with using a ruler and protractor, they should be able to complete the measurements quickly, leaving the majority of the time available for creating the chart and naming the triangles together. This part of the lesson can be completed in about thirty minutes. The portion of the lesson involving the building/architecture investigation and discussion can be completed in about thirty to forty-five minutes depending on whether all students use the same buildings or have different buildings to investigate. (total time: sixty to seventy-five minutes)

The second lesson is very similar to Lesson One but could take a little longer because students tend to be less familiar with solid figures. This lesson may take up to ninety minutes to complete and could be done over two days.

PROCEDURE

Lesson One

1. Give each student or pair of students a plastic bag containing pre-cut triangles of all three types (scalene, equilateral, isosceles) and ask them to examine them and then classify them in terms of their angles and

Figure 9.4   Sources for Objects: Geometry

Photographs work very well for this lesson and can be obtained from a variety of sources. Publications put out by many historical sites tend to have large, colorful photographs of their primary buildings and features. These photographs can be found in calendars, on postcards, or in inexpensive books or magazines. Look for those publications that are not only reasonably priced but also contain several photographs that can be used for the lesson. Paying $5.00 for a calendar may seem like a lot, but if you can get ten to twelve photographs out of it, it is well worth the money.

Many places also sell 3-D models of their buildings, which can also be used for this lesson. If you are artistically talented, you might take a photograph of a building and turn it into a 3-D model yourself using tag board and paint. A 3-D model allows students to better see the geometric solids found in architecture.

Finally, another money-saving way to collect these objects/photographs is to download images from the Internet. Many historical sites have excellent websites with color photographs of their buildings. I use the Colonial Williamsburg site to take my students on a "walking tour" of the colonial town and its buildings. There are drawings of many of the buildings that are ideal for use in analyzing the architecture.

---

side lengths. Make sure that the bags contain several examples of each of the three types and that all triangles are numbered or lettered for ease in identifying them.

Students will classify the triangles according to their own criteria, which hopefully will turn out to be the three types mentioned above. It is important not to introduce the terms or criteria for the different types of triangles until later in the lesson. Let the students discover the characteristics themselves and then name them together afterward.

2.   Give students time to use their rulers and protractors to measure the angles and sides of all triangles and to create their groupings. Walk around to ensure that all students are using the measuring tools correctly (this lesson assumes that these skills have been previously taught). Student should write down their observations about each triangle and be ready to explain their classification and the reasons for the groupings.

3.   Bring students back together for a discussion of the ways in which the triangles were alike and different from one another. Together create a chart on the blackboard filling in the information regarding the angles and side measurements. Finally, complete the name of the triangles by asking students to think about the most unique characteristic of that type of triangle.

Figure 9.5   Error Alert

> Measuring angles in triangles can be difficult for students. Check to ensure that students see the arm on which to line up their protractor and that they are using the correct row of measurement on the protractor. Having students first identify the angle as acute or obtuse prior to measuring is usually helpful with this error.

Figure 9.6   Name a Triangle

Name of Triangle	Acute Angles	Obtuse Angles	Right Angles	Equal Sides (Y/N)

4. Ask students where they have seen triangles in architecture (the faces of roofs, pediments, dormers, etc.). Tell them that this is the first lesson in an investigation of how geometry is used in architecture and that you will guide them through this first investigation. What types of triangles are used most often and most effectively in architecture?

5. Distribute pictures of buildings that use triangles in some way. Use pictures from books or actual photographs of buildings. Postcards are a good source of photographs. You could also tie this in with a social studies unit by using information from the Internet. Colonial Williamsburg, for example, has drawings of the colonial area buildings on their website. These could be shown on the TV or projection screen from a computer in your classroom for discussion and then printed out for students to use for measuring. You want the students to actually have these pictures on paper that is large enough to see, manipulate, and measure.

6. Have students work together to investigate the question regarding triangle use in architecture. They should measure the angles and side

Figure 9.7   Difficulty Alert: Measuring Angles

It is often difficult for students to use the protractors to measure angles in photographs of buildings. This is perhaps because it is a little more difficult to actually see the arms of the angle they are supposed to measure! I often highlight the angles for students who are having difficulty, using a different color for each angle. This makes it easier for students to see, and therefore measure, the angles.

lengths as before and compare their findings to the information in their charts.

7. Bring students back to discuss their findings. This is especially interesting if students have different buildings to analyze. You should see that some students will begin to see the connection to balance and harmony and some may even begin to make the connection to structural integrity.

DISCUSSION QUESTIONS

1. What are the similarities between triangle use and the types of triangles chosen in the different buildings?

2. Why do you think a particular type of triangle is used most often?

3. How does this choice affect aesthetic appeal? How does it affect the structural integrity of the building?

4. How can aesthetic "imbalance" still maintain structural integrity?

PROCEDURE

Lesson Two

Lesson One focused solely on triangles. Lesson Two is a lot like Lesson One, but it focuses on solid figures in comparison to plane figures.

1. Distribute sets of solid figures to groups of three to four students. Begin first by defining face and vertex/vertices. These two terms will be necessary for students to complete their investigation.

2. Have students create a chart like the one in Figure 9.8.

Figure 9.8   Recording Sheet for Solid Figures

Name of Figure	# Faces	# Line Segments	# Vertices	Drawing

Figure 9.9   Difficulty Alert: Keeping Track

> Students sometimes have trouble keeping track of which vertices and segments they have already measured. I sometimes have students affix a piece of Wicki Stix or highlighter tape to the segments they have already counted so that they won't repeat them. Students working together, though, can help each other keep track.

3. Give groups time to investigate their shape set and identify the information for columns two through five.

4. Go over the information together and have students brainstorm to complete column one, naming the figures.

5. Next, provide students with an opportunity to analyze photographs of buildings to investigate the following: *What geometric shapes are used most often and for what purposes?* I usually start by looking at a set of slides from Colonial Williamsburg, which has pictures of several restored buildings in the historic area. Many places have slide sets like this or have pictures on their websites. You might use slides of Frank Lloyd Wright designs, for example.

6. Bring students back together to discuss their findings. Tell them that one of their final tasks at the end of the unit will be a photography

Figure 9.10   3-D Objects

> This lesson is a good place to incorporate those 3-D building models simply because it is easier for students to see the solid shapes in them than it is in two-dimensional pictures.

assignment where they will have to do what they have just done—analyze a building—but for the project they will also be required to give reasoning as to why certain features might be used for specific purposes.

DISCUSSION QUESTIONS

1. What geometric solids are used most often in architecture?

2. What do you feel is the predominant reason that some figures are used more frequently than others? Aesthetics? Structural soundness?

3. What do you notice about the specific uses of certain figures? Are some used just for detail work/decoration? Others for foundation features?

4. How do geometric shapes enhance or take away from aesthetics? structural integrity?

COMMON FEATURES TO BOTH LESSONS

Adaptations

Use photographs of buildings from different time periods. How has triangle usage changed? What changes have occurred in the types of other geometric figures used? How can aesthetic "imbalance" still maintain structural integrity? You can have students trace architecture through the decades this way.

ASSESSMENT AND EVALUATION

The measuring and chart-making portions of the lessons are times for practice with the measuring tools and classification and should not be

Figure 9.11 "In this picture a balcony, dentil work, and dormer windows with pediments are featured. The balcony is made up of squares, rectangles, rectangular prisms, and circles. The dentil work is made up of rectangular prisms. The pediments above the dormer windows are made up of isosceles triangles which have two sides the same length, the third side longer, 2 acute angles, and 1 obtuse angle. I think they used this type of triangle for balance and because other types of triangles would make it uneven."—Samantha, 5th grade

evaluated. You should, however, assess which students still need help with the tools and which are comfortable using them, which students have greater difficulty with the classification task and which classify with ease.

The photograph analysis can be a time for further assessment of measuring tools and observation/analysis skills or, if done on a subsequent day, can be used as an evaluation.

The ultimate evaluation of students' understanding of (1) triangle types and usage and (2) plane versus solid figures comes in the final task when they are asked to use their understanding either to analyze a building or create one of their own.

Figure 9.12 "In this picture a cupola is featured. It is made up of squares and rectangles on the faces. They create a rectangular prism when they are put together. It also has a sphere on top of the cupola."—Samantha, 5th grade

Options

Photography/Building Analysis

• Work with your art teacher to develop a photography unit (or teach it yourself!). Many art teachers enjoy this type of art and can hook it in nicely with their objectives related to light and shadow or perspective.

Figure 9.13 "I decided to take a picture of this door because I thought it was unique. The door is a rectangular prism with a rectangle for the face and a line splitting in half making it symmetrical. There are also two more rectangles on each rectangular prism. These rectangles are split many times, making even more rectangles! I saw very few doors like this."— Emily, 5th grade

Figure 9.14   "This cupola represents a hexagonal figure. There is a weather vane on top of the cupola. Near the base of the cupola there is a balustrade. Below the balustrade there are many dormer windows with pediments. The dormers are triangular prisms and the faces are isosceles triangles. Each individual window has 15 squares, which are separated by perpendicular lines. This is clearly one of the more important buildings in the town."—Emily, 5th grade

- Give student groups (three to four students) a disposable camera to use on a class field trip. In the past I have done anything from the complex (taking my students to Colonial Williamsburg) to the simple (taking a walking tour around the town). It's best to have at least one parent volunteer per group so that groups can split up and more buildings can be featured.

- Have students take photographs (using the techniques taught by the art teacher) of different architectural features of the buildings that clearly utilize geometric figures they have studied. Students should remember to record on a piece of paper the picture number, photograph subject, and the student who took the picture so they will be able to claim their pictures after they are developed.

- Once the pictures are developed, have students analyze their pictures and write up an analysis of what features, both geometric and architectural, are seen in the photographs. They should also include some reasoning as to why they feel that these features do or do not work well for the building, both in terms of aesthetics and structural integrity.

Building Design

- Provide students with models of building designs done on chart paper so that they have a reference.

- Student groups should each be given a large piece of heavy chart paper on which to create their building.

- Groups should use construction paper, rulers, scissors, and glue to "construct" their home. It is important to remind students that while their building would contain solid figures, they must represent those figures as plane figures on the chart paper.

- Once the building is created on the chart paper, students should analyze their building and write up an analysis of what features, both geometric and architectural, are found in the design. They should also include some reasoning as to why they feel that these features do or do not work well for the building both in terms of aesthetics and structural integrity.

EXTENSIONS AND MODIFICATIONS

- Take students on a walk around the school to identify other uses of geometric figures in architecture. If the features are too high or too big to measure, have students brainstorm how they could determine what type of feature is being used.

- Invite a local architect into the classroom to discuss uses of geometry in architectural design. Make sure the architect also talks about how certain features enhance structural integrity.

- Work with your art teacher to have students create 3D models incorporating different geometric figures.

SUGGESTED READING

Burns, M. (1994). *The greedy triangle.* New York: Scholastic.
Neuschwander, C. (1997). *Sir Cumference and the first round table: A math adventure.* Watertown, MA: Charlesbridge.
Thomas Jefferson and architecture: Teacher resource packet grades 7–12. (1988). Charlottesville, VA: Monticello Education Department.

All other resources are dependent upon the area of history or architecture on which you want to focus. Choose books with large photographs of buildings that most clearly show the geometric features you want. For my unit, I focus on colonial Virginia and use resources such as historic Williamsburg postcard sets and calendars and the following:

Hatch, P. (1992). *The gardens of Thomas Jefferson's Monticello.* Charlottesville, VA: Thomas Jefferson Memorial Foundation.
Tate, T. (1996). *Williamsburg: A seasonal sampler.* Williamsburg, VA: The Colonial Williamsburg Foundation.

VOCABULARY

equilateral triangle: a triangle having all three sides the same length and three acute angles.

face: a flat side of a solid figure.

isosceles triangle: a triangle having two sides of equal length, two acute angles, and one obtuse angle.

plane figure: a geometric figure with only two dimensions—length and width.

scalene triangle: a triangle having no sides of equal length, two acute angles, and one obtuse angle.

solid figure: a geometric figure in three dimensions—length, width, and depth.

vertex: a point where line segments meet in a solid figure.

ACADEMIC STANDARDS

Grade Level: 5–8

Math:

Measuring angles and line segments, tool usage (NCTM 5–8.13 Measurement)

Identifying geometric figures and distinguishing between them (NCTM 5–8.12 Geometry)

Identifying real-life applications of geometry concepts (NCTM 5–8.12 Geometry)

Language:

Descriptive writing—analysis of photographs (ENG.K–12.4 Communication Skills)

Developing reasoning through writing (ENG.K–12.6 Applying Knowledge)

Social Studies:

Change over time—architectural style (NCSS Theme II—Time, Continuity, and Change)

Analyzing how perspective influences "style" (NCSS Theme I—Culture)

Art:

Concepts related to light and shadow (Consortium of National Arts Education Associations, Visual Arts 5–8.1 Understanding and Applying Media, Techniques, and Processes)

Concepts related to perspective and composition (Consortium of National Arts Education Associations, Visual Arts 5–8.2 Using Knowledge of Structures and Functions)

WHAT'S FOR DINNER?

ESSENTIAL UNDERSTANDING

Big Idea: Estimation

Essential Understanding: In many real-life situations, we need to be able to make reasonable estimates.

OBJECTIVES

Students will

- Estimate the cost of a meal by rounding decimal amounts.
- Add and subtract decimals (money) with regrouping.
- Order decimals.

MATERIALS

For this lesson you will need

- A collection of menus, available from local restaurants or the Internet
- Calculators (optional)

TIME REQUIRED

This lesson does not need to take a lot of time, especially for older students. Once they have the menu, deciding what to have is not difficult. Estimating costs of meals to the nearest dollar is also not time consuming. Usually, my students spend two forty-five-minute class periods to complete this project. The first period is spent on searching the menus for meals within their price range through estimation and then filling out the form. The second class period, which I hold in the computer lab, is used for creating the bill.

PROCEDURE

1. Tell students that they are going out to dinner with their parents. The school will pay for the dinner, but they can only have (give any dollar

amount) to spend on the three of them for dinner. They will be given a variety of menus, and they are to choose a place to go where the food is good, and it will fit their budget.

2. Students will be required to order drinks, an appetizer, a meal, and dessert for all three people. All three meals must be different. They will also be required to leave a 15-percent tip.

3. Hand out a variety of menus to each group of students. I like the students to work individually or in pairs for this activity. Menus can be traded and exchanged among groups to be sure there are a variety of choices.

4. Tell students they will need to estimate the cost of the dinner by rounding the cost to the nearest dollar. They should record their estimates, then using the calculator, find the actual cost of the dinner.

5. Once students come up with a reasonable estimate and a meal that fits their budget, they should calculate the tip.

6. Students will create the "bill" for their meal, which will include the tip. If possible, students can create this on the computer using a spreadsheet.

7. Worksheets and bills will be collected for evaluation.

DISCUSSION QUESTIONS

Students usually attack this lesson with a lot of independence and zeal. They love to order from restaurants. Younger students may have problems understanding percents, and you may opt to leave this out. However, I found my students quickly went to their calculator, found the percent key, and calculated the tip. This did not mean they understood the concept of percent though. To make this lesson more meaningful, after students have completed the activity, the following questions can be asked:

1. Why is it important to stay within your budget?

2. Why does it help to estimate the cost of a product before you purchase it, especially at a restaurant?

3. How do you calculate percents?

4. What is a percent?

Figure 9.15   What's For Dinner Organizer

ITEM	ESTIMATE	ACTUAL COST
Appetizer		
1		
2		
3		
Entree		
1		
2		
3		
Dessert		
1		
2		
3		
Drinks		
Total		
Tip		
Total With Tip		

Figure 9.16   Student Work Sample

Sergio's Italian Restaurant	
Appetizer	
Peancetta	$7.95
Insalata Mista	$5.25
Salomone Affumicato	$8.50
Drinks	
7up	$1.50
Lemonade	$1.50
Tea	$1.50
Entree	
Bistecca	$17.95
Peppercorn Encrusted	$17.95
Lemon Chicken	$9.00
Dessert	
Rum Cake	$3.95
Cheesecake	$4.50
Tiramisu	$5.25
Tip	$12.41
Total	$95.16

EVALUATION

Individuals or pairs of students will be formally evaluated on

- Making reasonable estimates to the closest dollar
- Staying within their budget by making reasonable estimates

EXTENSIONS AND MODIFICATIONS

- Menus could be downloaded from different areas of the United States. Students could find the average cost of dinner in each area and then compare costs. Graphs could be made to compare the cost of dining out across the country.

• This could be integrated into a unit on the five kingdoms in science by having students order something from each kingdom as part of their meal.

SUGGESTED RESOURCES

The Internet, for a variety of menus.

ACADEMIC STANDARDS

Grade Level: 4–8

Math: (National Standards)

Develop and use strategies to estimate computations involving decimals in situations relevant to students' experience (NM-NUM.3–5.3)

Develop and use strategies to estimate the results of computations involving decimals and to judge the reasonableness of such results (NM-NUM.3–5.3)

Work flexibly with fractions, decimals, and percents

WHAT PART OF FRACTIONS IS DIFFICULT?

ESSENTIAL UNDERSTANDING

Big Idea: In order to understand some math concepts, manipulatives need to be used.

Essential Understanding: Some concepts in the study of fractions are harder to understand than others. If students can teach the concept to someone else, then they will understand it too.

OBJECTIVES

Students will

- Explain a fraction concept they find difficult by drawing it out or through the use of manipulatives.
- Teach a difficult fraction concept to the class.

MATERIALS

For this lesson you will need

- A variety of manipulatives, including linking cubes, colored cards, fraction pieces, rulers, etc.
- Large drawing paper
- Math resource books
- Crayons, markers, or colored pencils

TIME REQUIRED

The time required for this lesson depends on how much time you want to give your students. I usually spend about twenty minutes talking about what the students are having trouble with, listing the concepts on the board, and then grouping the students. I let the students brainstorm as a group for about another twenty minutes. Some groups take longer than others. I then give them about another ninety minutes to research and then come up with a display to present to the class for the concept they are

Figure 9.17   Sources for Objects: Fractions

For this lesson, just about any collection of objects you have around the classroom can be used. When I do this lesson, I use fraction bars, beans, fraction strips, linking cubes, and anything else I can think of, or the students ask for.

teaching. Time to present the concepts will depend on the size of your class, but I usually reserve about four minutes per group for presentations.

PROCEDURE

This lesson is designed to help students get past a stumbling block in math. When my class was having difficulty grasping concepts dealing with fractions, I created this lesson, but the approach could be used for any math concept at any level.

1. Recognize that all students in the class are at different stages of understanding a concept being taught in math, such as fractions.

2. Discuss with the students what they are having trouble understanding.

3. Make a list of the problems on the board.

4. Going around the class, ask students to choose the concept they are having the most trouble with and place their name next to that concept on the board. These will be the groups that work together. If there are too many in one group, break it up into two or three groups. Also ask for students who think they are experts in one of the concepts a group is having trouble with.

5. Students will be instructed to use any manipulative they find in the classroom or on the supply table to teach the rest of the class the concept they have been having trouble with. Small group instruction may be needed to help some groups, but students should be given time to work with the manipulatives to come up with an explanation of their own. Students may ask other students or the teacher for advice or clarification of the concept. They may also use the Internet to "ask an expert," if necessary.

6. Students will prepare a lesson to present to the rest of the class. They may use manipulatives or draw the explanation on large drawing paper. They will practice giving the lesson to the rest of the group.

7. Revisions will be made as necessary.

8. Students will present the lesson to the class. Any graphic aids will be collected and assessed.

DISCUSSION QUESTIONS

Initially, it may sound like a bad idea to ask students who do not understand a concept to teach it to the class. However, it is a wonderful lesson in problem solving. It does teach the students about what they can do for themselves when they run into a concept they do not understand. It also forces them to look at the concept from a different point of view. Asking them guiding questions as they are needed helps students to focus in on the problem and find the resources necessary to understand the concept. Some of those guiding questions might include

1. Why is this concept so hard to understand?

2. What manipulative could you use to explain this concept to someone else?

3. Can you think of any time in your life when you use this concept? How could this help you teach this concept to someone else?

4. Would talking to an "expert" in this area help you to understand this concept? Can you turn around and teach this concept to someone else?

ASSESSMENT AND EVALUATION

Students will be informally evaluated as a group on

- Working cooperatively
- Staying on task
- Completing the task

The individual students will be formally evaluated for

Figure 9.18

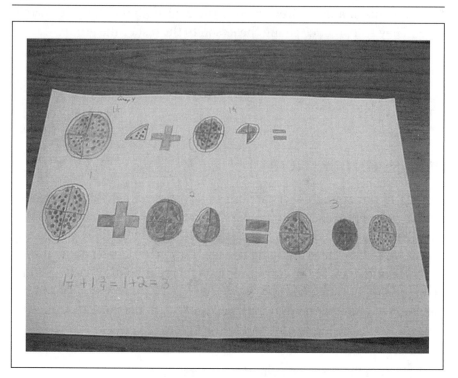

- Showing mastery of the concept through the lesson and communicating it to the rest of the class
- Oral communication skills

EXTENSIONS AND MODIFICATIONS

This lesson can be done with any math concept students are having difficulty grasping. It could also be used to introduce a unit that you have pretested and found that most students do not understand the concepts. In this case, you may just assign concepts, placing students who did not do well on a section together. This way, you could also do small group instruction where necessary.

SUGGESTED RESOURCES

Class experts on the concept, math textbook

Banfill, J. (2000). *Fractions*. AAA Math. Retrieved June, 2002, from http://www.aaamath.com/fra.html

Webb, B. J. *Fractions*. Kids' Online Resources. Retrieved June, 2002, from http://www.kidsolr.com/math/fractions.html

ACADEMIC STANDARDS

Grade Level: 4–8

Math:

Develop understanding of fractions as parts of unit wholes, parts of a collection, as locations on number lines, and as divisions of whole numbers (NM-NUM.3–5.1)

Use models, benchmarks, and equivalent forms to judge the size of a fraction (NM-NUM.3–5.1)

Develop and use strategies to estimate computations involving fractions (NM-NUM.3–5.3)

Use visual models, benchmarks, and equivalent forms to add and subtract commonly used fractions and decimals (NM-NUM.3–5.3)

Glossary

Adaptation: Change made over time to accommodate or adjust to one's environment

Alliteration: Repetition of consonant sounds (usually at the beginnings of words)

Artifact: Any object that represents something from the past and gives some information about a culture

Assonance: Repetition of vowel sounds (usually at the beginnings of words)

Biome: A community of plants and animals living together in a certain environment

Coniferous forest: Evergreen trees that produce cones and needles all year long

Distinguishing characteristics: The characteristics of something that makes it unique and different from other things

Equilateral triangle: A triangle having all three sides the same length and three acute angles

Excavation: The process of uncovering artifacts carefully from a site

Face: A flat side of a solid figure

Fantasy: A genre of literature with fanciful characteristics

Fringe: The part of the feather at the top that breaks up the flow of air and silences the flight

Genre: A particular style of literature with specific characteristics

Habitat: The environment something lives in

Hypothesis: An educated explanation of what you think something is or why you think something happened; hypotheses should be based on your past observations and experiences

Igneous rock: Rocks formed primarily through cooling magma; characterized by crystals and/or air pockets

Inner vane, outer vane: The part of the feather that faces away from the wind, and the part that faces into the wind

Isosceles triangle: A triangle having two sides of equal length, two acute angles, and one obtuse angle

Light zone: Physical depth of the ocean between approx. 0 and 320 feet, characterized by light, plant life, little pressure, and warmer water

Metamorphic rock: Rocks formed through constant heat and pressure over time

Midnight zone: Physical depth of the ocean greater than approximately 4,000 feet, characterized by no light, intense pressure, and freezing water

Node: The part of the stem where leaves begin to grow

Observations: Observations do not involve any reasoning; they are simply recordings of information you take in through your senses

Onomatopoeia: Words that are intended to represent a sound (e.g., buzzzzz)

Opposite leaves: A pair of leaves growing from the same node, one on each side of the stem

Perspective: Your point-of-view or the way in which you view things; based on your own experiences and beliefs

Plane figure: A geometric figure with only two dimensions—length and width

Rationale/justification: The reasoning that exists to back up something that is claimed or offered as a hypothesis

Region: A geographic area differentiated from other geographic areas by particular land or water features, climate, and resources

Resources: Natural or man-made objects used in the production of some other object or tool

Rubric: Specified guidelines for what particular levels of performance should look like or be like

Scalene triangle: A triangle having no sides of equal length, two acute angles, and one obtuse angle

Sedimentary rock: Rocks formed through layering of sediments that become pressed/cemented together over time

Shaft: The part of the feather in the middle that holds the fringe

Solid figure: A geometric figure in three dimensions—length, width, and depth.

Twilight zone: Physical depth of the ocean between approximately 600 and 3,200 feet, characterized by dim blue light, higher levels of pressure, and colder water

Vertex: A point where line segments meet in a solid figure

Index

**CORWIN
PRESS**

The Corwin Press logo—a raven striding across an open book—represents the
happy union of courage and learning. We are a professional-level publisher of
books and journals for K-12 educators, and we are committed to creating and
providing resources that embody these qualities. Corwin's motto is "Success for
All Learners."